Christian Heroes: Then & Now

# John Williams

## Messenger of Peace

I0821961

CHRISTIAN HEROES: THEN & NOW

# JOHN WILLIAMS

## Messenger of Peace

JANET & GEOFF BENGE

YWAM Publishing is the publishing ministry of Youth With A Mission (YWAM), an international missionary organization of Christians from many denominations dedicated to presenting Jesus Christ to this generation. To this end, YWAM has focused its efforts in three main areas: (1) training and equipping believers for their part in fulfilling the Great Commission (Matthew 28:19), (2) personal evangelism, and (3) mercy ministry (medical and relief work).

To learn more about our books and materials, call (425) 771-1153 or (800) 922-2143 or email books@ywampublishing.com. Visit us online at www.ywampublishing.com.

**John Williams: Messenger of Peace**


Published by YWAM Publishing
a ministry of Youth With A Mission
P.O. Box 55787, Seattle, WA 98155



Library of Congress Cataloging-in-Publication Data
Benge, Janet, 1958–
John Williams, messenger of peace / Janet and Geoff Benge.
p. cm. — (Christian heroes, then & now)
ISBN 1-57658-256-6
1. Williams, John, 1796–1839. 2. Missionaries—Polynesia—Biography.
I. Benge, Geoff, 1954– II. Title. III. Series.
BV3672.W5 B46 2002
266'.58'092—dc21 2002002644

ISBN 978-1-57658-256-5 (paperback)
ISBN 978-1-57658-619-8 (e-book)

Sixth printing 2025

Printed in the United States of America

# Christian Heroes: Then & Now

Adoniram Judson
Albert Schweitzer
Amy Carmichael
Betty Greene
Brother Andrew
Cameron Townsend
Charles Mulli
Clarence Jones
Corrie ten Boom
Count Zinzendorf
C. S. Lewis
C. T. Studd
David Bussau
David Livingstone
Dietrich Bonhoeffer
D. L. Moody
Elisabeth Elliot
Eric Liddell
Florence Young
Francis Asbury
George Müller
Gladys Aylward
Helen Roseveare
Hudson Taylor
Ida Scudder
Isobel Kuhn
Jacob DeShazer
Jim Elliot
John Flynn
John Newton
John Wesley
John Williams
Jonathan Goforth
Klaus-Dieter John
Lillian Trasher
Loren Cunningham
Lottie Moon
Mary Slessor
Mildred Cable
Nate Saint
Norman Grubb
Paul Brand
Rachel Saint
Richard Wurmbrand
Rowland Bingham
Samuel Zwemer
Sundar Singh
Wilfred Grenfell
William Booth
William Carey

*Available in paperback, e-book, and audiobook formats. Unit study curriculum guides are available for select biographies.*

*www.YWAMpublishing.com*

*In memory of my mother,*
*Shirley Hilda Crombie*

*1933–1990*

*This book combines two of her great loves:*
*her Lord and the Pacific islands.*

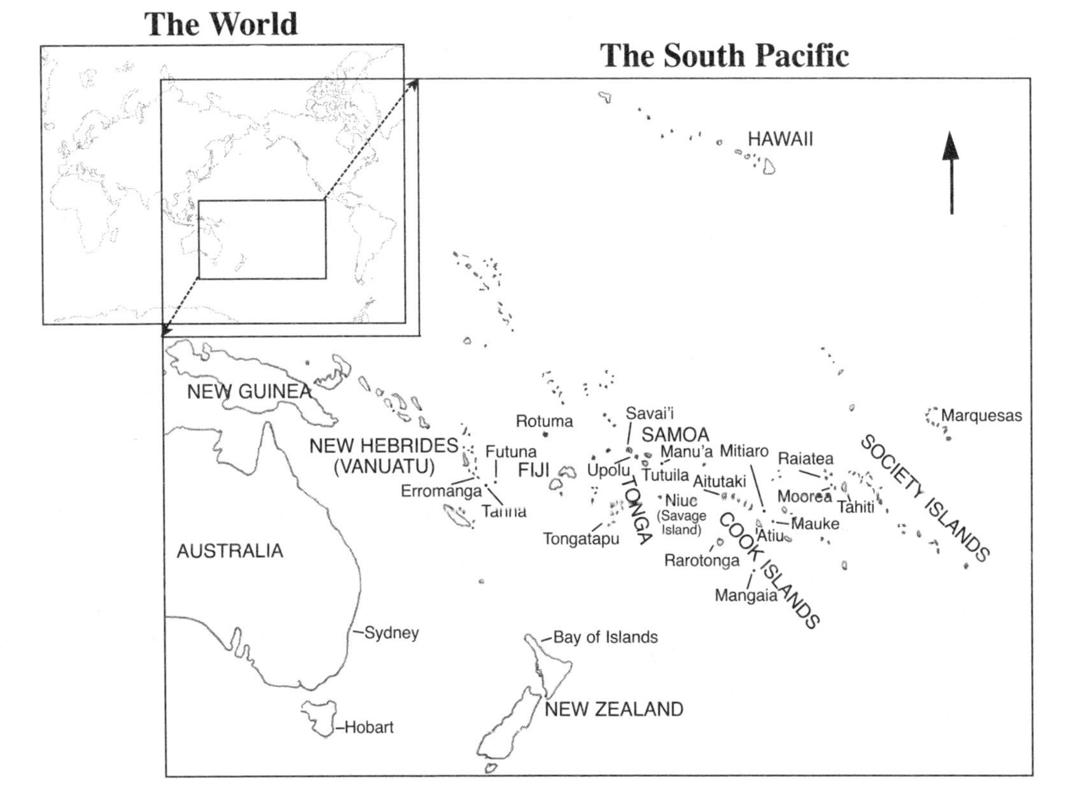
The World
The South Pacific
HAWAII
Marquesas
SOCIETY ISLANDS
Raiatea
Tahiti
Moorea
Mauke
Atiu
Mitiaro
COOK ISLANDS
Mangaia
Rarotonga
Aitutaki
SAMOA
Savai'i
Manu'a
Tutuila
Upolu
Niuc
(Savage Island)
TONGA
Tongatapu
Rotuma
FIJI
Futuna
Tanna
Erromanga
NEW HEBRIDES
(VANUATU)
NEW GUINEA
AUSTRALIA
Sydney
Hobart
Bay of Islands
NEW ZEALAND

# Contents

1. Our Father Is Alive! . . . . . . . . . . . . . . . . . . . 13
2. The Best Hour of His Entire Life . . . . . . . . . . 17
3. The Long Voyage . . . . . . . . . . . . . . . . . . . . 29
4. A New Home . . . . . . . . . . . . . . . . . . . . . . . 41
5. Raiatea . . . . . . . . . . . . . . . . . . . . . . . . . . 53
6. Links in a Chain . . . . . . . . . . . . . . . . . . . . 67
7. The Endeavour . . . . . . . . . . . . . . . . . . . . . 77
8. Rarotonga at Last . . . . . . . . . . . . . . . . . . . 89
9. Messenger of Peace . . . . . . . . . . . . . . . . . . 99
10. Questions . . . . . . . . . . . . . . . . . . . . . . . . 115
11. A Change in Plans . . . . . . . . . . . . . . . . . . 127
12. Samoa . . . . . . . . . . . . . . . . . . . . . . . . . . 139
13. A Time to Rebuild . . . . . . . . . . . . . . . . . . 151
14. A Day of Turning . . . . . . . . . . . . . . . . . . . 161
15. Old England . . . . . . . . . . . . . . . . . . . . . . 171
16. They Have Killed Our Father! . . . . . . . . . . . 185

Bibliography . . . . . . . . . . . . . . . . . . . . . . 197

Chapter 1

# Our Father Is Alive!

"I will return soon!" John Williams yelled to the Atiu islanders as he waded into the lagoon and climbed aboard the rowboat, taking his place at the stern.

Two tattooed Polynesian men heaved on the oars in unison, and the boat began to cut its way across the calm, crystal-clear water. John turned to wave to his island friends, who were now singing a traditional farewell song. The words drifted across the lagoon to him as he thought about his first encounter years before with the people of this island. Back then their chief, Roma-Tane, had regularly ordered children to be sacrificed and enemies cooked and eaten in honor of the many gods they worshiped. They also robbed and starved the first missionaries who came to work among them. But now they called their island Lotu—given to God. Now there was a thriving Christian church on Atiu, and Polynesian teachers from the Society Islands taught the people to read and write.

Slowly the singing from shore was drowned out by the thunderous crash of breakers on the coral reef that surrounded the island. The Polynesian rowers were maneuvering the boat through a gap in the reef when one of them yelled, "Hold on!"

John whipped his head up to see an enormous freak wave descending on the rowboat. The craft was quickly upended, and before he could grab ahold of anything, John was flung into the surging water. He gasped one last breath as the force of the wave pulled him under. Frantically he thrashed his arms and kicked his legs, but it was no use; the undercurrent was too strong. His lungs throbbed for air as he felt himself being pulled farther downward.

*I can't drown! I can't drown! There are too many islands to go! I have to reach them all!* John told himself over and over as he fought the urge to breathe.

He kicked harder and harder, and slowly, very slowly, he felt himself begin to rise. Suddenly his head burst through the surface. He opened his mouth, and air exploded into his lungs. After several deep breaths, he looked around to get his bearings. The ship they were headed for lay in the distance, and the capsized rowboat was bobbing near the reef about twenty yards away.

John could see the two rowers swimming for shore. Still sputtering, he began swimming after them. His nose and throat burned from the salt water.

Wham! Another huge wave crashed over John. This time it hurled him forward onto the coral reef. "God help me!" he prayed as he felt his left leg being torn open by the sharp coral. He knew that many men, even expert Polynesian sailors, had perished on the reefs, where they were dragged under by the waves and trapped in the many caverns and fissures. Before drowning, their flesh was ripped to shreds on the razor-sharp coral.

John could not let that happen to him. Once again he frantically kicked and thrashed as he tried to get away from the jagged reef. But with each burst of effort, the current pushed him back. John's strength was beginning to fail when two sets of strong arms surrounded him.

"Rest on us. We will get you to shore."

John looked around to see two Atiu men, one on either side of him. He felt their powerful legs kick, and slowly they all moved away from the danger of the reef and into the calm, safe water of the lagoon. The men pulled John along until he felt sand beneath his feet.

"Our Father is alive! Our Father is alive! We thought you drowned, but you are alive!" cried the Atiu Christians as they ran to help John up onto the beach. Many of them kissed his hands and laughed with joy.

As he rested on the beach after the ordeal, John wondered how he could ever explain to his friends back in England the adventures he had experienced since coming to the South Pacific. In fact it was difficult for him to believe some of his adventures. He now lived in such a different world from his friends and from the life he had known as an apprentice back in London.

Things could all have been so different if he had not met Mrs. Tonkin on the street that Sunday night so many years ago. Without that seemingly chance meeting he could be back in England plying his trade as an ironmonger instead of being halfway around the world proclaiming the gospel among cannibals and fierce warriors.

Chapter 2

# The Best Hour of His Entire Life

Seventeen-year-old John Williams stood outside the bakery on City Road in London waiting for three friends to show up. It was Sunday, January 3, 1814, and church bells were chiming six o'clock in the evening. "Trust them to be late!" John murmured to himself, trying to think what he should do next. Should he go on without his friends or waste more time waiting? The four of them were supposed to be going to Highbury Tea Gardens, which sold more beer than tea. The other three boys, like John, were apprentices, and each Sunday night they enjoyed drinking at Highbury Tea Gardens and swapping stories from work.

"Oh, John, how good to see you," came a female voice from behind him.

John turned to see who it was. He quickly pulled off his cap. "Mrs. Tonkin, ma'am," he said, unsure what else to say to the wife of his employer.

"I am glad I ran into you, John," Mrs. Tonkin went on. "I have been wanting to invite you to come to church with me for quite some time, and now look, you are standing on the side of the road doing nothing, and I am on my way to church not two blocks from here!"

John smiled nervously. The last thing he wanted to do was set foot in a church. His mother was a Christian, and she had dragged him to church with her every Sunday when he was a boy. Now that he was out from under her grasp, he had no intention of wasting part of his day off on such a boring activity. Church was fine for women like Mrs. Tonkin and his mother, but it certainly was not anything he was interested in.

John looked up and down the street, hoping to catch a glimpse of one of his friends, but no one was in sight. "Uh, thank you, Mrs. Tonkin," he replied gingerly. "I would be happy to go to church with you one day, but not today, as I am waiting to meet some friends. We are going to do something together."

"And where might you be going?" Mrs. Tonkin asked.

Now John felt trapped. Being an apprentice in 1814 was a serious matter. His employer had control over where he went and what he did, even on days off. If John said he was going to a beer garden, he might get in trouble with Mr. Tonkin, and he couldn't think of a good lie to make up on the spot.

"Oh," he said, "we weren't going anywhere. We were just meeting here."

Mrs. Tonkin gave him a questioning look. "Well," she said, linking her arm into John's, "then you really don't have anywhere else to go, and I think Mr. Tonkin would be very pleased to hear that his fine young apprentice accompanied me to church tonight. What do you say?"

What could he say? John forced a feeble smile and nodded. Five minutes later the two of them were walking through the doors of Whitefield Tabernacle. Mrs. Tonkin led the way to a pew near the front and sat down triumphantly.

Once seated in the hard pew, John readied himself for the long, monotonous sermon he knew would be coming. Sure enough, after several hymns and a prayer, the Reverend Timothy East walked to the pulpit. His voice was deep and clear. "I have taken for my text tonight the passage from the Gospel of Mark, chapter 8, verses 36 and 37. 'For what shall it profit a man, if he shall gain the whole world, and lose his own soul? Or what shall a man give in exchange for his soul?'" he began.

John intended to daydream his way through the sermon, but there was something about what was being said that kept rousing his interest.

"What is there in this world that is worth exchanging your soul for?" the Reverend East asked.

The words struck John like a shaft of light in a darkened room. What was there in his life that was worth exchanging his soul for? A night at a beer garden with his friends? His ambition to one day be a rich iron merchant? The hope of having a pretty girlfriend? All of these things seemed shallow when weighed against eternity.

In an instant, as the Reverend East continued on with his sermon, John Williams made a decision—he was headed down the wrong road in life, and he was going to change direction right there and then. It was time he became a Christian. He had felt frustrated and intimidated by his employer's wife when he walked into the church. When he left an hour later, he was convinced he had just spent the best hour of his entire life!

During the weeks that followed, John Williams was determined to change his behavior. He traded going to beer gardens for attending Bible studies, going to church, and visiting the sick. Within two months he was even teaching a Sunday school class.

John knew some co-workers at the ironmongery made fun of his new faith and behavior, but he did not care. Let them laugh. He had found something worth living for. Other people noticed his zeal, too, and soon the Reverend Matthew Wilks, assistant pastor at Whitefield Tabernacle, invited John to join a special class he was holding. Called the Mutual Improvement Society, the class consisted of a group of young men who met together each Monday night to discuss ways to prepare themselves to become pastors. John was not quite sure whether that was the right direction for him. Being a pastor sounded a little beyond his few years of formal schooling, but since he was eager to improve himself in any way he could, he went along to the society meetings.

One night, about two years later, the Reverend Wilks talked to the young men about something that sent John's heart racing. "I have in my hand a wooden object, as you can all see," he began, holding up a carved figure about eighteen inches tall. "This object is a symbol of both missionary endurance and God's faithfulness. You have all heard me talk many times about the London Missionary Society and the first group of missionaries it sent out on the *Duff* twenty years ago. Thirty missionaries were on board, destined for one of the most remote and unknown regions on earth—the Pacific islands. Few missionaries had been there before, though a rough assortment of traders, whalers, and escaped convicts from New South Wales infested the islands, plying the natives with rum and guns. The *Duff* put missionaries off at Tahiti, Tonga, and the Marquesas. Eventually murder, sickness, and discouragement reduced their number to only three of the original missionaries, including Henry Nott, a stalwart ex-brickmaker who would not give up the battle for native souls. God guided him to befriend King Pomare of Tahiti, and when the king died, his son King Pomare II also came to regard Mr. Nott as a worthy friend. Now we have received word that

King Pomare II has turned his heart toward God and wishes to become a Christian."

Once again Matthew Wilks held up the carving. "This," he continued, "is one of twelve idols that were the personal property of King Pomare II. He has sent it all the way to England to show Christians here that he is serious about the desire to put away his evil practices."

John had often heard the Reverend Wilks talk about the London Missionary Society, or LMS, as it was known, and its goal of bringing Christianity to the Pacific islands. But staring at this idol carved by human hands and worshiped as a god drove the urgency of that goal home to him.

"We must all pray diligently for the people of Tahiti and for Henry Nott. For hundreds of years the islanders have practiced infanticide, ritual killing, and cannibalism. Now alcohol and guns have made matters worse. Without God these people are doomed," the Reverend Wilks said emphatically.

That night, and for many nights afterward, John prayed for the Tahitian people and for King Pomare II. And every time he prayed, he felt the same goose-bumpy feeling run through his body. As he thought about Henry Nott, the ex-bricklayer, and the work he was doing, it occurred to John that perhaps he too could become a missionary.

John continued to turn the idea around in his head until finally he could not keep it to himself anymore. He felt he would burst if he did not confide in someone. After church one Sunday he spoke with

Matthew Wilks about the idea. He was very grateful when the Reverend Wilks did not laugh at him but instead asked him questions.

"You are apprenticed, are you not?"

"Yes, sir," John replied. "My papers were signed in March 1810, so I am free to seek other employment in 1817."

"Hmm, that's still a year away. But why don't you apply to become a missionary anyway, and if you are accepted, we will see what we can do about your apprenticeship papers."

"Do you really think I have a chance?" John inquired, trying to keep his hopes in check.

The Reverend Wilks nodded. "I can't promise anything, but I am on the LMS board, and I can personally vouch for your steadfast Christian character and service, and I must say, we are looking for young men and couples to go and take advantage of King Pomare's openness to the gospel. Come to my office with me, and I will get you an application."

John hardly slept the next week. His mind raced with thoughts about missionary work. However, as he wrote and rewrote his answers to the questions on the application, he was concerned that he might not seem impressive enough. Actually, he had to admit to himself that he did not look impressive at all!

He had been raised in nearby Tottenham, where he had gone to school for several years to learn writing and arithmetic. But that was as far as his education had gone, and in the spaces on the application marked "College" and "Degrees Earned," John had nothing to write. The blank spaces discouraged him, until he thought of Henry Nott, who as a bricklayer probably did not have much more formal education than he had.

In the end John decided not to try to make things sound any fancier than they were. He wrote, "In offering the following representation for your perusal I have endeavored to be as frank and plain as possible. If this, and the account which the Rev. Mr. Wilks can give of me, should not meet with your conscientious approbation [approval], I hope, pray and trust that you will, on no account, for the sake of my soul, offer me the least encouragement." He then went on to list the church activities he had been involved in since his conversion: visiting the sick, handing out tracts, teaching Sunday school, and attending the Reverend Wilks's self-improvement classes.

Much to John's surprise, his writing was substantial enough for the board of the London Missionary Society to grant him an interview. At the interview, which was held on August 5, 1816, John answered as best he could a barrage of questions on everything from his opinion of the previous Sunday's sermon to how to conjugate English verbs. The following week he was asked to attend a second interview, after which Matthew Wilks informed him that he had been accepted as an LMS missionary.

John could scarcely believe it. The mission director himself had told him that the LMS did not have the funds to accept everyone who applied to be sent out by them, and so they only accepted those missionary candidates who showed the most promise.

From the moment John was accepted to be a missionary, things began to change rapidly for him. John told his employer about his new plans, and Mr. Tonkin offered to release him from the remaining months of his apprenticeship in exchange for thirty pounds. The LMS agreed to pay the price, and now there was nothing stopping John from going out as a missionary. He did, however, have something else on his mind. He knew there were very few, if any, single Christian women in the Pacific islands, and so he decided it would be best to marry before he left so that he could take a wife with him. But who could or would be his wife?

There was only one answer in John's mind—Mary Chawner. The Chawner family had been members of Whitefield Tabernacle for many years, and they took an active interest in missionary endeavors. Lately John had noticed that Mary sounded particularly interested in missionary work herself. Of course there was no way she could go out as a single woman and be a missionary, as such a thing was not allowed. But she could go as the wife of a missionary, and John began to wonder whether the two of them would make a good team. He liked Mary. She was petite, had sparkling green eyes and a ready smile, and seemed to have an easygoing way about her. But how could he ask her to give up her family and friends and accompany him on a dangerous mission with no certain outcome? John decided to wait.

Meanwhile other aspects of his new calling were moving along at top speed. It was normal for the LMS to require its missionary candidates to undergo training at a seminary, but with the urgent need for workers in both the Pacific islands and Africa, that requirement was waived. Instead John met for private lessons with the Reverend Wilks and attended several classes with the other eight candidates who were to be sent out at the same time. It would then be up to the London Missionary Society board to decide where the men should go, though the candidates were allowed to suggest their preferences.

During this time John struck up a friendship with one of the other candidates, a burly Scottish man named Robert Moffat. The two were the same age, and Robert had just finished his apprenticeship as a gardener. As the two missionary candidates discussed their plans, they found that they thought very much alike and so asked for permission to be sent to either destination together.

Much to John's disappointment, the Reverend William Roby, director of the LMS, told them they could not team up because they were the two youngest candidates and each needed to be under the wing of an older man.

On September 30, 1816, the nine missionary candidates were dedicated in a special missionary service at Surrey Chapel. The first five men who were called to the altar were all bound for Africa; Robert Moffat was among them. The other four men, John, David Darling, George Platt, and Robert Bourne, were commissioned to go to the Pacific islands. As the men were dedicated for their new calling, Dr. Waugh, who was leading the service, walked along the line of men and spoke to each one separately. John looked into his fiery eyes as he said, "Go, my dear young brother, and if your tongue cleaves to the roof of your mouth, let it be with telling poor sinners the love of Jesus; and if your arms drop off at your shoulders, let it be with knocking at men's hearts, to gain an entrance for Him there."

A month later, on October 27, twenty-year-old John Williams stood at the altar again, this time with Mary Chawner at his side. He had gathered all his courage and asked her to marry him, and she had agreed. The couple stood saying their wedding vows just twenty-one days before the *Harriet* was due to set sail on November 17, 1816, and transport them from the only world they had known to a Polynesian kingdom almost halfway around the world.

Chapter 3

# The Long Voyage

John Williams stood on the poop deck of the *Harriet* and breathed deeply. Salt-laden air filled his lungs. As he slowly expelled the air, John thought about how much he loved being at sea. The cry of the gulls circling overhead, the splash of the waves against the side of the ship, the creaking of the rigging as the sails strained against the gentle but steady breeze and pulled the ship forward—they were all sounds that seemed so natural to him now. Even the gentle pitch and roll of the ship beneath his feet felt normal.

The movement of the ship had not had the same effect on John's wife, however. Mary was below deck, stretched out in the cabin seasick. She had looked terrible when John went below to check on her. Her face was ashen and her eyes sunken. But he could do nothing for her. "She'll find her sea legs soon enough," the captain had told him. John hoped that Mary found them soon so that she could leave the fetid atmosphere belowdecks and join him on deck to bask in the sun and breathe the fresh salt air.

John took several more deep breaths before heading belowdecks again. This time he did not go to the cabin to check on Mary. Instead he descended into the bowels of the ship until he was standing on the very bottom of the hull. In dim light John felt his way around, observing how the ship was constructed. He was especially interested in the way iron spikes were used to hold the planks and beams together to form the hull.

John was glad that the captain had given him permission to look around belowdecks. After every foray to observe how the ship was put together, he took notes and drew sketches of the various construction techniques he had observed. John had no idea why he was doing this, other than to pass the time and satisfy his ironmonger's curiosity as to how things were made.

It wasn't just how the ship was put together that fascinated John. He was also interested in the various sailing techniques, especially tacking, which allowed the captain to maneuver the ship forward even in a head wind. He also asked the captain question after question about navigating and how he fixed the position of the ship. The captain showed John a sextant and patiently explained how he used it to fix his latitude—his north-south position—from the stars at night and from the rising sun in the morning. He also showed John the extremely accurate chronometer set to Greenwich time that he used to establish his longitude—his east-west position. With these two instruments the captain could fairly accurately pinpoint his position on a map.

One morning the captain rolled out a map in his cabin and showed John the route they would follow on the voyage. They were on their way to Rio de Janeiro, Brazil. After taking on supplies there, the *Harriet* would follow a southeasterly course across the southern Atlantic Ocean, around the Cape of Good Hope at the tip of Africa, across the Indian Ocean, and on to Tasmania. After a stop in Hobart, Tasmania, they would head north to Sydney, New South Wales. There the missionaries would change ships to the *Active* for the trip eastward across the Pacific Ocean to the Tahitian islands. And using the readings he had taken that morning, the captain calculated the position of the ship and showed John where they were on the map. They were approximately halfway to Rio de Janeiro.

Five weeks after leaving England, Mary had found her sea legs, and she and John stood on the deck of the *Harriet* and watched as Rio de Janeiro appeared on the horizon. It was a beautiful sight. The city was nestled on the edge of a bay surrounded on the north and west by rocky, forested mountains. A long strip of gleaming white sand beach stretched south from the city as far as the eye could see. An unusual jagged rock formation protruded skyward from a point that jutted into the bay. "*Pão de Açúcar,* or Sugarloaf," the captain said, pointing to the rocky landform.

John and Mary could hardly wait for the *Harriet* to drop anchor in Guanabara Bay so that they could go ashore and explore the first foreign country either of them had ever encountered.

Before they even set foot in Rio de Janeiro, however, John and Mary's impression of the place was tarnished. Three miles from the city a ship sailed past, headed in the opposite direction. John could make out fifty or more nearly naked black people on board, all chained together. The wailing of the women carried across the water to the *Harriet*. The vessel was a slave ship, and John supposed it was headed for the Caribbean. He squeezed Mary's hand tightly until the cries of the women aboard the slave ship trailed off into the distance.

Finally the *Harriet* sat at anchor in Guanabara Bay, and John and Mary were rowed ashore in a longboat. Once ashore they strolled through the narrow streets of the city until they found themselves in a large, open-air market filled with vendors selling every imaginable thing. John was particularly enthralled with the variety of tropical fruits and vegetables for sale, many of which he had never seen before. Dogs scampered around, and voices and music and laughter rose with the pungent odor of the market to fill the air. It was all so different from England.

Then John saw something else that was very different from England—a slave market. The sight of groups of African men, women, and children, their hands and feet manacled and chained together in groups of about twenty, sickened him. The slaves sat on narrow wooden benches, waiting to be sold. The sorrow etched into their sunken eyes and their blank stares seemed to reach out and grab John.

Soon afterward John and Mary returned to the ship, but John could not get the image of the slaves in the market out of his mind. He had to do something. He could not be silent in the face of such injustice and suffering. So the missionary men went back to the market and found a corner on which to preach.

"Friends," John began, "it is with great sadness that I observe a horrible blight on the beautiful land God has blessed you with. And that blight is slavery."

"Keep your mouth shut!" yelled someone from a nearby banana stall.

"No one asked for your opinion!" ventured another vendor.

John stood his ground. "Every one of you will have to give an account to the living God for the way in which you treat other human beings." Just then John saw something flashing to his left. He turned and saw a man holding a butcher's knife lunging toward him.

"We don't need the likes of you telling us how to live!" the man yelled.

John ducked and managed to slip past his attacker. He scampered into a nearby cobblestone street and ran as fast as he could. He could hear the butcher-knife-wielding assailant close behind as he turned into a narrow, twisting alley. Several minutes later John was out of breath and lost, but at least the man was no longer chasing him. Sobered by the experience, John eventually found his way through the crowded streets back to the dock where the longboat from the *Harriet* was tied up.

Waiting by the longboat, where he had expected to catch up to the other missionary men, who had also fled the scene, was a man John had never seen before but who somehow seemed to know who he was. "Hello, friend. Let me introduce myself,"the man said, holding out his hand for John to shake. "I'm Lancelot Threlkeld, and you must be John Williams."

The two men shook hands and then sat down on a couple of nearby wooden crates, where John told Lancelot about his close call at the slave market. Lancelot understood completely. He and his wife, Martha, had been bound for Tahiti as LMS missionaries on an earlier ship, but Martha had become too sick to go on. As a result they disembarked and stayed on in Rio de Janeiro so that Martha could recover and await the next ship headed for the Pacific. During this time, he told John, he too had been sickened by the slave trade and would have stayed on in the city and tried to change things if he and Martha had not already pledged themselves to serve in the Tahitian islands. The Threlkelds would be sailing on the *Harriet* with the others when the ship left Rio de Janeiro.

Once fresh provisions and water were brought aboard, the *Harriet* again set sail. It headed in a southeasterly direction toward the Cape of Good Hope. This leg of the voyage proved to be much rougher than the westward trip from England to Rio de Janeiro, and longer too—a normal crossing took over three months. John spent much of his time on board studying the Bible, praying, and talking to the other missionaries about what they should do when they eventually arrived at their final destination. Of course none of them had much idea about what to expect. They had never seen a Pacific islander and had little idea about what life would be like in the islands. Lancelot told them that on his trip out to Rio de Janeiro he had gotten to know another LMS missionary, named William Ellis, who was a printer by trade. William had brought with him a simple printing press and a supply of paper and had planned to start printing Bibles in the various dialects spoken in the islands. This sounded like a wonderful idea to John, who hoped that he could be a part of distributing the Bibles around the region.

By mid-March 1817 the *Harriet* was lying at anchor in Hobart, Tasmania, having crossed the South Atlantic and the Indian Ocean. Hobart was a small but thriving port that serviced whalers and merchants. John and Mary went ashore with the other missionaries, and what they saw was no more encouraging than what they had seen in Rio de Janeiro. This time, though, it was not slavery that held the people in bondage but alcohol. It seemed to the missionaries that beer and rum flowed as freely as water. When they met the governor of Tasmania, who was returning from a hunting expedition, he was drunk and singing nursery songs to a puppy that was cradled in his arms. The pastor of the only church in the settlement was no better. He could barely stagger to the pulpit to preach on Sundays, and his speech was so slurred it was hard to understand what he was saying.

After a brief stay the *Harriet* sailed north toward Sydney, New South Wales, where they would disembark. They hoped to connect with the *Active,* a ship the London Missionary Society chartered to transport missionaries from Sydney to the various Pacific islands.

On May 12, 1817, six months after leaving London, the *Harriet* dropped anchor in Sydney Harbor. Soon after they arrived, a brawny man of about fifty was rowed out to the ship. He introduced himself as the Reverend Samuel Marsden, the LMS representative in New South Wales and the senior chaplain of the Botany Bay penal colony. The Reverend Marsden invited the missionaries to stay with him while they waited for the *Active* to return from a trip to Tahiti. It took two days to offload all of the missionaries' cargo and store it in a warehouse. Once this was done, there was little else to do but wait for the *Active* to appear in the harbor.

John Williams, however, was not a man to sit around drinking tea and gossiping. He wanted to learn everything he could about this new land he had arrived in. He often spent his days with Samuel Marsden, watching what he did and asking a thousand questions. It didn't take him long to work out that Samuel was a powerhouse of activity and ideas.

Samuel explained to John that the War of Independence in America had meant Britain was no longer able to send convicts to jails in Virginia. Soon British jails were overflowing, and something had to be done. That was when someone suggested that the land surrounding Botany Bay would be a suitable location for a penal colony, and in 1788 the first ships carrying convicts arrived. The Reverend Marsden had then come out from England to be chaplain of the colony. He took John on a tour of a model farm that the convicts had developed under his supervision, and the two men visited several mission schools that educated both the convicts and their children.

Perhaps the endeavor that Samuel Marsden was the most passionate about was the New South Wales Society for Affording Protection of the Natives of the South Sea Islands. Samuel had founded the society four years earlier after hearing about the terrible treatment being meted out to natives by whalers, sealers, and traders. These men routinely cheated the natives, plundered their natural resources, abused the women, and, if they had a mind to, murdered the population of whole villages or islands. Through his society, Samuel Marsden hoped to agitate for change and a humane approach to dealing with the natives. The islanders needed to be seen and understood as people and not just as a hindrance to exploiting the natural resources of the region.

The missionaries waited anxiously in Sydney, but it was not until late August that the *Active* finally showed up. After a group of convicts unloaded the vessel, the missionaries' cargo, including a number of bars of iron and a set of bellows John had brought with him so that he could set up a forge and do some ironwork, was put aboard.

Finally, on September 2, 1817, the missionaries were ready to embark on the last leg of their journey. Another missionary couple, Charles and Sarah Barff, joined them for the voyage, bringing the number of missionary men on board the *Active* to six, three of whom—John Williams, Lancelot Threlkeld, and Charles Barff—were married.

John hoped for Mary's sake that it would be a fast and calm trip to the Tahitian islands. She was expecting a baby sometime around Christmas. John's hopes were quickly dashed when the *Active* ran into a vicious storm. For several days the ship was lashed by gale-force winds, until one of her masts snapped. Nineteen days after setting out from Sydney, the *Active* limped into the Bay of Islands near the northern tip of North Island, New Zealand. Repairs were made to the ship, and a new mast of *kauri,* a New Zealand hardwood, was fitted.

The Bay of Islands intrigued John. By now it was October, autumn in London but spring in the southern hemisphere. The breeze that blew across the bay was warm, and the vegetation on the surrounding countryside was lush. Along the seashore a particularly gnarled variety of trees, ablaze with red flowers, seemed to thrive.

Before the missionaries made it ashore they encountered the local native population, the Maoris. For the first time, John was seeing Polynesian people. The Maoris paddled out to the ship in their canoes and scrambled aboard. They poured onto the deck of the *Active* and greeted the missionaries with their customary rubbing of noses. Their skin was brown, and they had wavy black hair. John was amazed at how friendly they were despite their fearsome looks, especially the men, who had swirling tattoos that covered almost every square inch of their face. The captain of the *Active* told John that Maori facial tattoos were unique among the people of Polynesia.

After their encounter with the Maoris, John and Mary and the other missionaries went ashore and were greeted by members of the Church Missionary Society who had set up the first mission station in New Zealand just four years before. Even now these missionaries did not dare venture far from the shoreline. The Maoris, despite their friendly greeting aboard the *Active,* had a reputation for being the fiercest natives in the Pacific. The various tribes were constantly making war on each other.

To make matters worse, escaped convicts from New South Wales settled among them, gladly helping them plot more effective ways to annihilate each other and organizing with the whaling ships to import guns for that purpose. These white advisors also did all they could to stir up the Maoris to chase away the missionaries. They did not want missionaries interfering with the life they had carved out for themselves.

Finally, after several days at anchor in the Bay of Islands, repairs to the *Active* were completed and the ship got under way again, carrying John and Mary closer to their new home.

Chapter 4

# A New Home

On Monday, November 17, 1817, exactly one year after setting sail from England, John stood on deck and watched his new home come into view. The island of Moorea lay just west of the main island of Tahiti. Its jagged peaks rose from the deep, blue water of the Pacific Ocean. Thick vegetation covered the island, whose glistening beaches were bordered by towering coconut palms. Around the whole island lay a coral reef, against which the waves crashed, throwing foam into the air and creating a thunderous roar. Inside the reef the water was calm and powder blue. It was an amazing sight and more beautiful than anything John had imagined.

The late morning sun was high overhead as the *Active* sailed along the eastern side of the island.

From his perch on deck, John could see the island of Tahiti several miles off the starboard side of the ship. Though Tahiti was a bigger island, John thought Moorea was the more spectacular island of the two when seen from the water.

As the ship sailed along, a gap opened in the reef and the captain headed the ship into it. The *Active* slipped into a small natural harbor, where it dropped anchor.

On shore was a small village, which the missionaries later learned was called Afareaitu. Once the *Active* was safely at anchor, long canoes manned by muscular Polynesian men glided out from the beach to greet the visitors. The missionaries climbed over the side of the ship and down a rope ladder into the canoes bobbing alongside. Several minutes later they were all standing on the edge of the island's gleaming white sand beach, the crystal water of the lagoon lapping at their feet.

Waiting on the beach to meet them were three LMS missionaries stationed on Moorea—William Ellis, the printer, and John and Margaret Orsmond. They invited everyone, including the *Active's* captain and crew, to a meal before the unloading of the ship began. As John sat on the beach, most of the food put in front of him was foreign. Large slabs of fish, yams, coconuts, and breadfruit were all washed down with very weak tea.

"We are hoping you have brought more tea with you," laughed William. "As you can see, we are making the most of the little we have left."

John smiled. "I believe we have tea packed in the hold," he assured William.

Palm trees swayed in the breeze, and the smell of native flowers filled the air. As the missionaries and the crew of the *Active* ate their meal, the local people stood around watching. The women wore long, white, shapeless dresses like nightgowns, while the men had a length of cloth wrapped around their waist. Many of the men also had rings through their noses and tattoos on their arms and legs.

It took the remainder of the day to unload all the cargo from the *Active.* The ship's captain was eager to be on his way again, as the trade winds were due to die down anytime now and he wanted to be well on his way back to Sydney by then.

Five sailors who had traveled on the ship to Moorea with the missionaries would also be staying on the island. These men had been sent by Samuel Marsden, who had heard that King Pomare was building his own ship and had engaged the sailors to crew the vessel.

That night John and Mary and the other newly arrived missionaries slept in a long hut made of woven coconut fronds. John hardly slept at all. His mind was alive with ideas about how he could reach the Polynesians.

The next morning, after a time of prayer and a Bible reading, John Orsmond asked the new arrivals to go with him and look at the frame of the seventy-ton boat that King Pomare and the missionaries had begun work on the year before. The task had become too difficult to complete, and the project had been abandoned. Now the half-built vessel lay on its side on a nearby beach. The idea for the boat, John Orsmond explained, had been to use it to collect pearls and mother-of-pearl from the nearby Tuamotu Islands to ship to New South Wales, where the cargo could be exchanged for items the islanders needed, such as knives and tools.

John Williams, along with the five sailors and the other new missionaries, had spent the previous two and a half months aboard the *Active* with little else to do but talk, pray, and read. Now that they were ashore, they were looking for some kind of physical challenge and thought they had found it in the abandoned hull of the ship. They decided that between them they could complete the project. John agreed to make all the iron fittings for the ship, but first he had to set up a forge, which he would build on the beach near the boat.

After gathering a pile of rocks, John began to stack them together in a circle to form the forge. He left a small opening near the bottom through which his bellows would blow air to get the temperature of the coals in the forge high enough to make the iron red-hot so that he could mold and shape it. As John worked, a group of local men watched his every move.

Soon John became frustrated at this, not because the locals were watching him but because he could not talk to them in their language. William Ellis told him that the Polynesian language was difficult to master. He had made slow progress learning it in the time he had been on Moorea and estimated that it would be three years before he could speak it fluently, studying each night from the Tahitian grammar and spelling book that early LMS missionaries had prepared.

The thought of waiting three years before he could speak directly to these people made no sense at all to John. Surely there had to be a faster way to learn the language. As he hammered away shaping iron into spikes, pulley wheels, and the other various pieces of hardware needed for the new boat, John thought about the problem. As a child he had learned English from those around him by listening to what they said and repeating their words, even if he made mistakes that sounded funny. Why not apply the same approach to learning Tahitian? John started right away. He pointed to the sand, a man, a baby, a tree, gesturing to whoever was nearby to tell him the native word for the thing. The locals understood right away what he was doing. John soon found that he was never alone. Some curious Polynesian was always at his elbow repeating simple words to him and laughing at his attempts to imitate them. John laughed too. He knew how funny his pronunciation must sound to them, but he did not give up.

Everyone was surprised at the progress the men made on the boat. After languishing on the beach for nearly a year, the vessel was ready to launch two weeks after the newly arrived missionaries began work on it. King Pomare was invited to come over from the island of Tahiti to see the boat launched. John was eager to finally meet this man he had heard so much about.

King Pomare II arrived in a large outrigger canoe, escorted by an entourage of warriors in smaller canoes. Henry Nott accompanied King Pomare from Tahiti. John wished he could have captured the scene and sent it to the Reverend Wilks and the young men in the Mutual Improvement Society back at Whitefield Tabernacle in London. Here in front of him were the two men they had all heard so much about.

With great pomp and ceremony, King Pomare was carried ashore from his canoe and set down on the beach. John marveled at the feat, given the size of the king. King Pomare was a huge man, tall and wide. His long hair was tied back into a ponytail, and he had a wispy moustache and small tuft of beard on his chin. He wore black trousers and a pleated white shirt.

Once safely ashore, King Pomare announced that he had decided to name the new boat the *Hawies,* after Dr. Thomas Hawies, the founder of the London Missionary Society and a man the king had heard a lot about. The launching ceremony began with a prayer by Henry Nott. The locals then manned ropes on both sides of the ship to keep it upright as they slid it down a makeshift slip into the water.

John watched proudly as King Pomare stood at the bow of the vessel and declared, "I name this ship the *Hawies.*" Then, as he had been instructed, the king swung a bottle of wine against the hull. The bottle shattered, and the ship toppled onto its side! The rope holders had been so surprised by the wine bottle breaking that they let go of the ropes and fled. It took all the men in King Pomare's entourage helping to get the *Hawies* upright once again and into the water. A huge cheer went up from the crowd when the vessel finally sat floating in the lagoon.

Now that the boat was finished, John turned his attention to building a simple house for himself and Mary and the soon-to-arrive baby. When not working on building the dwelling, he spent his time listening to and imitating the language. Soon he was able to speak in simple sentences.

On January 7, 1818, John Chawner Williams was born. He was strong and healthy, and his parents were both very proud of him. A constant parade of islanders came to stare and laugh at the "pink" baby.

Soon after the birth of the baby came the birth of the Tahiti Missionary Society, the local branch of the LMS, which was to be run and funded by Tahitian Christians themselves. The goal of the society was "making the Word of God grow" in the islands. The idea of Polynesians taking an active role in running their own missionary society was new, and everyone waited anxiously to see how it would work out.

The society had a strong beginning. King Pomare was made its president and proudly announced that he and his wife had prepared arrowroot with their own hands as an offering to the society. Other offerings of pigs and coconut oil began to pour in. Soon the Tahiti Missionary Society had five hundred pounds of goods to ship on the *Hawies* to Sydney, where the cargo could be sold to provide money.

Everything was going well—too well, really. In John Williams's opinion there were too many missionaries huddled on the islands of Tahiti and Moorea when there was so much more work to be done on nearby islands. John longed to go somewhere new—somewhere that did not already have a well-established missionary base. His opportunity to go to such a place came in June when several chiefs from the nearby island of Huahine invited the missionaries to set up a station there. They had seen the mission's work on Tahiti and Moorea and now wanted missionaries working among them.

John and Mary quickly volunteered for the new venture, along with fellow LMS missionaries John and Margaret Orsmond, William Ellis, and John Davies. The local mission leaders approved their move, and the group soon was packed and ready to go. Of course, the printing press and forge went along as well. And the group took livestock, including five goats that would produce milk for their tea.

On Huahine the missionaries were given an enthusiastic welcome, along with gifts of pigs, native cloth, and all kinds of local fruit. Mary was delighted with the reception and quite willing to live with John and the baby in a thatched hut the locals provided them. John was grateful for his wife's happy temperament and her faith that things would work out. He knew how blessed he was to have someone such as Mary who did not complain and beg to go home.

John and the other missionaries busied themselves setting up a mission station, and John continued to work hard learning the language. All of the other missionaries were working through a laborious grammar and lexicon that Henry Nott had hastily put together for them, but John still believed it was better to listen and talk with the Polynesians themselves. The method worked for him, and by September, only ten months after setting foot in the islands, he was able to preach his first sermon in Tahitian. Now he was ready for a new challenge!

This challenge came in the form of Tamatoa, the chief of the island of Raiatea. All the missionaries in the Society Islands, the island group of which the Tahitian islands were a part, knew about Raiatea. It was the center of a large religious group who worshiped the god Oro. Polynesians came from other places to offer human sacrifices and worship at the island's *marae,* the wide stone platform where religious rituals were performed. But something amazing had happened on Raiatea, even before a single missionary had set foot on the island.

Chief Tamatoa had been exposed to Christian teaching several years before while visiting Tahiti. He and many of his warriors fought alongside King Pomare as the king struggled to regain control of the island after a rebellion had broken out. The Tahitian Christians the chief met at this time impressed him, and before long Tamatoa decided to abandon the worship of Oro and the other gods and become a Christian. Many of his warriors joined him in the decision. But when they returned to Raiatea, their new faith provoked outrage from those they had left behind.

To explain why he had given up his traditional gods, Tamatoa toured the island with his family, meeting with people. During this time he invited his wife to sit and eat pork with him. This caused an outrage because pork was a sacred food that men could eat but women were forbidden to touch. Such action would only provoke the wrath of Oro, and everyone on the island waited to see what would happen to Tamatoa's wife. To everyone's surprise, nothing happened, and soon all of the women in Tamatoa's party were eating pork.

The women then asked to be allowed to eat turtle. This was even more outrageous than their eating pork. Turtle was the most sacred food of all. Again, when the women ate it, nothing happened. Finally, some of the chief's servants had taken shelter from a storm in an idol house. They had gotten cold, and recalling the way the women had broken taboos about eating pork and turtle, they had taken a length of cloth that was wrapped around an idol and used it as a blanket. This insult to their gods was too much for the people who worshiped Oro on Raiatea. They mounted a surprise attack on the chief and his Christian followers. Even though Tamatoa was greatly outnumbered, he and his men managed to win the fight. However, instead of killing and eating those who had attacked them, as was normal practice, Tamatoa and his men allowed their attackers to go free. This turn of events startled the attackers, and soon a number of them were asking about this new God who had more power than Oro.

This was just the kind of opening John had been looking for. On September 11, 1818, just days after meeting Tamatoa, the Williamses and Lancelot and Martha Threlkeld, who had agreed to settle with them in Raiatea, climbed into canoes to be paddled into unknown territory.

## Chapter 5

# Raiatea

Not everyone was happy with the missionaries' move to Raiatea. Some of those who were the least happy about it were the more experienced missionaries in Tahiti. They warned John and Lancelot of the dangers involved in going out on their own among the local Polynesians, especially since both of them had been in the islands for less than a year. And while John spoke passable Tahitian, Lancelot still had a long way to go before he could make himself properly understood in the language.

Nonetheless the two missionaries would not be held back. This was why John had come to the Pacific. Despite the risks, they would not turn down an invitation to extend the reach of the gospel to the

Oro worshipers of Raiatea, especially since there were plenty of other missionaries to carry on the work they had been engaged in.

The canoes carrying the missionaries headed west from Huahine, and eventually the jagged outline of Raiatea appeared on the horizon. From the water the island looked very much like Moorea, with its razorback rocky peaks, lush vegetation, and surrounding coral reef. The boats maneuvered their way through a gap in the reef and were soon floating in the crystal-clear water of the lagoon.

When the canoes pulled up on the beach, the local Christians welcomed the missionaries. They laid at the feet of these new visitors stalks of bananas and plantains, along with a pig and several fish, still warm from being cooked in the *umu,* or underground oven. They then led the Threlkelds and Williamses, with John Jr. propped on Mary's hip, to their tiny huts. The place still smelled of the freshly cut coconut fronds that had been woven together for the roof and walls. The floor was compacted dirt, which John promised to cover with a layer of crushed coral.

Upon their arrival on the island, the missionaries set right to work. They had already decided on a schedule. They would spend each Monday, Tuesday, and Thursday taking care of practical matters, such as teaching the locals new skills, including how to use tools. Wednesdays, Fridays, and Saturdays were set aside for writing and practicing sermons in Tahitian. Sunday, of course, was for a range of Christian meetings. Five services were held that day, the first starting at 6 a.m. and the last one ending at 4 p.m. The missionaries then ate dinner together and held their own service in English. The other evenings were busy, too, with a weekly meeting at which the Raiateans were free to ask the missionaries any questions they wanted.

The schedule was a great idea. There was just one problem—people didn't come to the events. The people of Raiatea lived in scattered huts all over the island. Before the arrival of the missionaries, the constant threat of attack by other tribes had made it unwise for the Raiateans to live together in villages. In many cases getting to Va'oara Beach, where the two missionary families had set up their mission station, was a major trek and not one the people wanted to make each day. Besides, the islanders appeared to have little idea of time. No one had a watch or a clock. Rather, people's daily life seemed to be delineated by the rhythm of the tides and the changing direction of the wind.

Something had to be done. John, Lancelot, and Tamatoa called a conference of the people, and it was decided that a village should be built beside the beach at Va'oara. Now John had a project he could get to work on. He decided to build himself a house and use it as an example of what a man could do with knowledge and a few local materials. He began right away, laying the foundations for a seven-room villa he had been planning in his head.

Each day many locals came to watch John work. They held the saw and exclaimed over its sharp teeth. They imitated John using his square to place the walls at right angles and the way he notched the poles that would hold the roof before he lashed them with rope. Soon a fine building began to take shape. It was sixty feet long and thirty feet wide, with a veranda that overlooked the lagoon.

Once the frame was up, John filled in the walls with slatted wood and then embarked on an experiment: making plaster from coral. To do this, he built a large fire and heated chunks of coral. When the coral cooled, he ground it into sand, which he mixed with water to make a chalky white plaster. The Polynesians stared in amazement as he daubed the plaster onto the walls. The experiment worked wonderfully, and the house was then completed with a thatched roof, which the local people helped him make.

Once the mission house was finished, virtually everyone on the island made the journey to see it. And just as John had hoped, many of those who saw the place determined to build their own house on the beach at Va'oara.

Missionary reinforcements soon arrived in the form of John and Margaret Orsmond, who had heard of the village project and wanted to come and be a part of it. The Orsmonds brought with them several hundred newly printed portions of the Gospels in the Tahitian language.

Now, with houses being built and a community taking shape, the missionaries were ready to teach the Polynesians how to read. This proved surprisingly easy, mainly because of the enthusiasm with which the Raiateans threw themselves into the task. School was held at noon Monday through Friday, and everyone from the oldest warrior to the youngest child who could sit still attended. The people were astonished as they learned to read and write simple messages on trays filled with sand.

These first months of work in Raiatea were clouded by the death of Margaret Orsmond after a short illness. The missionaries used her death as a reminder that they had a lot more work to do. None of them knew how much longer they had to live among the Raiateans.

In May 1819 news came that King Pomare II of Tahiti had been baptized in an enormous wooden church built in honor of the event. The church was named the Royal Mission Chapel, and at 712 feet long and 54 feet wide, it was big enough to hold six thousand people. Many members of the fledgling church at Raiatea had paddled over to witness the event, and they came back fired up with enthusiasm for building a similar church at Va'oara. John promised to start drawing up plans for such a structure, but since there were only about two thousand inhabitants on Raiatea, he told the travelers that the church would be built on a much smaller scale than the chapel in Tahiti.

That month mail arrived from England. It was the first mail the Williamses had received since arriving in the Pacific islands eighteen months before. John excitedly opened the letters, although his excitement soon turned to frustration when he opened a letter from the director of the London Missionary Society. Dated July 1818, it was obviously a circular letter sent to all the missionaries serving in the Society Islands. The letter read:

> The Society cannot allow itself to enter into any engagement with regard to the ownership or employment of the vessel now built or being built by the missionaries in the South Sea Islands and that the directors recommend them to dispose of her in the best manner you are able, in whatever state or place she may be on the arrival of this communication.

John was so shocked by the letter that he didn't trust himself to speak. The *Hawies* was being put to good use ferrying missionaries and supplies between the islands. What did the LMS directors think they were doing? Not one of them had ever been to the Pacific islands and had little idea of the challenges the missionaries faced getting around. And the fact that it could take up to two years from the time a letter was sent until a response was received meant that the constantly changing conditions made many of the demands carried in such letters outdated.

By now John had been in the islands long enough to know two things. First, ships were vital to the work of missionaries in the Pacific. The islands were like English villages, only they were connected not by roads and paths but by water. Just as missionaries serving in large countries needed carts and carriages to get around, the missionaries living in the islands needed a way to cross the ocean that surrounded them. On a continent, if all else failed, a missionary could walk to the next village. But in the islands one could not swim to the next group of islands.

The second thing John knew was that he was not the type of missionary to build a single mission station and then spend the rest of his life making sure it ran efficiently. He had a restless streak and was always wondering what unevangelized islands lay over the horizon. As far as John was concerned, using ships to spread the gospel was a vital part of any mission plan in the South Sea islands. And he was not prepared to give up the use of such a vessel at the whim of a mission board located on the other side of the world in London.

Alas, John had little say in the matter. The senior missionaries, led by Henry Nott, agreed to do as the mission board directed, and the *Hawies* was soon sold.

After the sale of the boat, John's attention returned to his work, and in September he sent his first report back to England. It was a year since he had moved to Raiatea, and he had much to report. The village of Va'oara now stretched for two miles along the beach, and the Raiateans were eager to learn new skills. John wrote in his report:

> We are going to attempt a large clock and wooden smith's bellows almost immediately.

> Our various little works of this kind, our boats and our houses have given the natives many new and important ideas. These they readily receive and act upon, and it is with delight I observe them engaging in the different branches of carpentering, some box-making, some bedstead-making, some making very neat sofas (which we have lately taught them) with turned legs and looking very respectable indeed, some again lime-burning, some sawing, some boat-building, some working at the forge, and some sugar-boiling; while the women are equally busy in making gowns, plaiting bark, and working neat bonnets—all the effect of the gospel…I have lately taught a native to bind books, which he can do very well.

By the beginning of 1820, the people of Raiatea were ready to take on the challenge of building their own chapel. The plans John had drawn up called for a structure smaller than the one in Tahiti, but at 191 feet long and 44 feet wide, it was still large enough to hold everyone on the island. Work on the building progressed fast, and on May 11, 1820, two thousand people turned out for the dedication service. The Auxiliary Missionary Society of Raiatea was formed, too, with Chief Tamatoa as its president. Soon seventy Raiateans were baptized.

There were other promising signs as well. As these Polynesians became Christians, they wanted laws, something they had never had before. Tamatoa called a meeting at which the islanders began discussing the laws they wanted. In the end a court system was set up, with Tamatoa's brother as the judge and the back of the chapel partitioned off to serve as a courthouse.

Many of the Raiateans were very happy with the changes taking place on their island. For the first time ever, the women and children were safe, and the men were not constantly at war. But some of the people resented the shift in power away from the native priests and the god Oro to the missionaries. Within weeks of the chapel's completion, John Williams found out just how determined these people were to rid the island of the missionaries' influence.

John was sitting in his chair preparing a sermon one Friday afternoon when he heard a knock at the door. Normally he would have gotten up and answered it, but as he was in the middle of translating a particularly difficult Bible passage into Tahitian, he called for one of the Raiatean women helping Mary prepare dinner to answer it. (Mary was expecting another baby in two months and needed help with the housework.)

Just as John called out, a commotion erupted outside. "Turn out the hog! Let us cut his throat!" a man yelled from the other side of the door.

John jumped up and barred the door. Mary came rushing into the room. "What is it, John?" she asked in a trembling voice.

"I don't know," he replied. "You sit down and pray. I'll take care of it."

John crept up to the window and peeked out. Standing on his veranda were two large men. One was wearing a pair of trousers as a jacket, an arm stuffed into each leg. John's heart skipped a beat when he saw the machete the other man was brandishing.

"Come on out, you pig!" goaded the man with the machete. "I'm going to cut your throat."

Mary sobbed quietly as John backed away from the window. What should he do? There was no back way out of the house, and the two men were much larger than he was.

Just then John heard singing. He looked out the window again to see a group of six Christians walking up his path carrying a string of fish. When the would-be murderers saw them approach, they leaped off the veranda and ran away.

John flung the door open to welcome his friends. They had saved his family from certain death. Mary, however, took a long time to calm down after the incident. In fact, she was so upset that their baby came early. It died within hours of being born, and the Williamses buried it beside the new chapel.

Despite the loss of their baby, John and Mary were reminded in a celebration held at the school that the Christian message had saved the lives of hundreds of other babies. By 1821 three hundred children and many adults were regularly attending the missionary school. The teachers decided to have a parade and had the children make banners that expressed why they were grateful to be able to learn to read and write. Several of the children decorated a banner that read, "Had it not been for the gospel we should have been destroyed as soon as we were born."

When an old man in the crowd saw the banner and learned what it said, he asked Tamatoa for permission to speak to the gathered crowd.

"Oh, that I had known that these blessings were in store for us!" he began. "Then I would have saved my children, and they would have been among this happy group repeating these precious truths. I shall die childless, though I have been the father of nineteen children."

John did not doubt what the old man was saying. Before the missionaries arrived with the gospel, most of the children born on the island were killed soon after they were born. The native priests told the people that the god Oro demanded they sacrifice the thing that was the most precious to them. Since the mothers loved their babies, the babies were taken away and sacrificed at the *marae*.

While the parade of so many eager and happy children made John feel proud, it also made him feel strangely restless. He felt that his work on Raiatea was over, and he knew that there were other missionaries and local Christians who were more than capable of continuing the church work. It was time for him to move on.

But where should he go? John realized that he would never be content to spend his life on a single island, and the LMS board had now taken away the *Hawies,* the only efficient means of traveling from one island to another. As he thought about it, he decided to write to the mission board in London and request a transfer to Africa or somewhere else where there was a larger population to work among. In his letter he wrote:

> I have given myself wholly to the Lord.... I have not another desire but to live and die in the work of my Saviour...but I regret that I ever came to these islands.... I request, then, a removal.
>
> The reasons which induce me to request a removal are, first, the small population of this island, and the comparatively easy life I am now living.... Our settlements consist of from 600 to 1,000 persons, and our congregations about the same; and there are at Huahine three missionaries and three at Raiatea.
>
> I saw in your publication that there were 34,000 inhabitants in these islands.... There were only 5,000 or 6,000...in Tahiti with 8 or 9 missionaries, I naturally expected to find about 28,000 persons in the six leeward islands....After two years of travelling...I can find about 4,000 inhabitants. I know that one soul is of infinite value. But how does the

> merchant act who goes in search of goodly pearls? Supposing he knows where there is one pearl...and at the same time, another spot, where there are thousands of equal value; to which would he direct his way?

John did not intend to wait a year or two for a reply to his letter. He started making plans to leave as soon as the next boat arrived. Sure enough a boat did arrive, just not the one he was expecting.

Chapter 6

# Links in a Chain

A cooling breeze blew in from the ocean as John Williams strolled along the beach one morning in March 1821. The tops of the coconut palms that lined the shore rocked gently from side to side above him, and the perfectly transparent water of the lagoon lapped at his feet while gulls dived and turned overhead. But John was oblivious to it all. His mind was on the letter he had just written requesting a transfer and wondering where he might be sent next—Africa, he hoped, where his friend Robert Moffat was serving. As he walked and thought, something on the horizon caught his attention. He stopped and looked out to sea, narrowing his eyes and putting his hand above them to shield against the glare of the morning sun. As he looked, he could see it was a large outrigger canoe. Lined up along her side a group of warriors were paddling rhythmically as they guided the vessel toward Va'oara. Quickly John turned and began heading back down the beach toward the village.

By the time he reached Va'oara, the canoe had entered the lagoon and was just a few hundred feet from shore. A large crowd had gathered to watch as the strangers came ashore. About twenty-five people were in the canoe, and one man, who appeared to be their chief, jumped out of the canoe and waded ashore. "I come in peace," he said.

John and Chief Tamatoa stepped forward to welcome the stranger.

"My name is Auura, and I am the chief of Rurutu," the stranger continued as the rest of his party pulled the canoe ashore. "Many days ago a terrible sickness came to our island. Many of our number died. We believed the gods were punishing us and were determined to kill us all. So my brother chief and I each built the biggest canoes we could, filled them with our people, and paddled into the deep. We were on the water for many days, and food and fresh water were no more. Then a violent storm overtook us, and my brother's canoe was swallowed up by the waves and seen no more. After twenty days we spied an island within a coral reef. We were driven up onto the reef by the waves, and some men from the island paddled out to help us. They told us their island was called Maura, and had we not reached Maura then, we surely would have perished."

The chief stopped to take a breath, and John noticed with pride that a mat had already been spread on the sand and the local Raiateans were piling cold taro and breadfruit on it for the weary travelers to eat.

The chief continued with his explanation. "The people of Maura were very kind to us. We were astonished when they showed us their *maraes,* all broken down, and their idols turned to ashes by their own hands. 'Who are you to destroy your gods?' I asked them. 'And what terrible things have befallen you as a result?'

"'Nothing bad has happened,' they replied. 'In fact, great good has come upon us. We now worship one God who does not have a wooden form, nor does he require the sacrifice of human flesh.'

"These things truly amazed us, and we stayed with them for some time, waiting to see when the gods would send punishment, but they never did. Soon we asked about the new God they served, and they instructed us that there were white people on other islands like this one who would tell us more and show us the way to the God who makes them happy and kind toward strangers."

As John listened to Chief Auura, he became more and more excited. He could see that he had not given himself enough time to really understand what his role could be as a missionary in the South Pacific. There was plenty of work to do here, and for him it did not have to involve running one little mission station on one little island. No! He realized that he could teach the local Polynesians themselves to take the gospel to the other islands, from the Society Islands all the way across the Pacific to Australia, like links in a giant chain. Christianity could be spread for thousands of miles across the ocean by dedicated local missionaries, each of whom need go no farther than to his neighboring island.

Tamatoa, Chief Auura, and John continued to talk as everyone ate and drank. Then the Rurutuans were given a grand tour of Va'oara, including the schoolhouse, with which they were most impressed.

"So this is where you teach people to say aloud the things that are drawn on paper," Auura said. "I would like to learn how to do that now."

John laughed. There was nothing like an eager student!

Over the following weeks John found that Auura was not only eager but also very intelligent. In less than three months he had mastered the Tahitian spelling book, could repeat the basic catechism of Christian beliefs, and could read the Gospel of Matthew! And several of the other members of his party were not far behind him in their learning.

"Once I thought I would never return, but now I am very anxious to revisit my own island," Chief Auura told John. "I wish to carry to those of my relatives who are still alive the knowledge of the true God and His Son Jesus Christ."

Within a week of this request, a ship stopped at Raiatea. Captain Grimes, the vessel's master, was a strong supporter of the LMS and had stopped to pick up a cargo of coconut oil that the islanders had produced under the missionaries' direction. John asked the captain if he would be willing to divert a little on his journey to England to return the Rurutuans to their island three hundred miles to the south. On hearing the circumstances, Captain Grimes readily agreed to transport the group back to Rurutu.

When Auura heard of the captain's kind offer, he looked downcast. "How can I go to a land of darkness without a light in my hand?" he lamented. "Will you send someone with me who has more knowledge of the one true and powerful God than I do?"

Instantly John knew what he should do. He must put the request before the Christians of Raiatea and see whether they would rise to the challenge.

That evening after dinner, the village drummers beat out the news that a special church meeting was going to begin. When a good number of the congregation had arrived, John explained to them that Auura wanted to go back to his own island but that he wanted Christian teachers to go with him. Who, John challenged them, would take the good news to their neighbors?

Two men, both well-respected deacons in the church, stood up. "Here we are," they said. "Send us."

So it was settled. The first official Raiatean missionaries were commissioned and sent off with Captain Grimes, Chief Auura, and the rest of those who had arrived with him. The Christians of Raiatea promised to pray for them every day.

Before long the Raiatean Christians were eager to know what was going on in Rurutu. They decided to send some of their best seafarers off in their canoe to visit the two deacons. The men arrived back jubilantly a month later. "The kingdom of God has come to the people of Rurutu," one of the men declared as they pulled their canoe up onto the beach.

"See, they have forsaken their idols, and our brothers are teaching them how to read the Holy Book," said another of the men, waving a wooden statue in the air.

A meeting was called immediately, and eager Christians gathered to hear news of their missionaries. The returning seafarers displayed many idols, including one of the god Aa. The statue had a small chamber carved in its back that stored twenty-four lesser gods. Letters written by the two deacons were produced and read. They filled the Christians with delight, not only because they told the story of how the local people were opening their hearts to the gospel but also because they told of events far away. Before they had learned to read and write, the Raiateans had no way to communicate with each other except by beating certain drum patterns or through talking. Now, with writing, words could be put on paper in one location and read in another location three hundred miles away!

John, along with everyone else, was stirred within as the letters were read, and more so when Tamatoa stood and gave his response. "Let us continue to give our oil and arrowroot to God," he said, "that the blind may see and the deaf hear. Let us not be weary in this work. We behold the great deep: it is full of sea; it is rough and rugged underneath; but the water makes a plain, smooth surface, so that nothing of its ruggedness is seen. Our lands were rugged and rough with abominable and wicked practices: but the good word of God has made them smooth. Many other countries are now rough and rugged with wickedness and wicked customs. The word of God alone can make these rough places smooth. Let us all be diligent in this good work, till the rugged world is made smooth by the word of God, as the waters cover the ruggedness of the great deep. Let us, above all, be concerned to have our own hearts washed in Jesus' blood; then God will become our friend, and Jesus our brother."

The two deacons' success in Rurutu gave the church a new sense of energy and purpose. Within weeks five hundred people presented themselves to be baptized, and John began planning how to send more of them out as missionaries. He wondered how he could have ever thought there was not enough work for him to do in the Pacific! Now he saw every island as a possibility. According to Chief Auura there were other islands around Rurutu, one of which he said was called Rarotonga. The name stuck in John's mind, and he determined that one day he would go there himself.

Ironically, soon after John discovered his true calling of teaching and sending out Polynesian missionaries, he became convinced that he would have to leave the islands. This time it had nothing to do with his wanting to give up, but rather it had to do with his health. For the past two years he had noticed his arms and legs swelled up from time to time, but now they were constantly puffy and red. He sometimes found it hard to walk and had to sit for hours with his legs propped up on a chair. He wasn't sure what was wrong with him, but he knew he had to go to Sydney, New South Wales, to seek medical attention before the condition got worse.

Just as John was making plans to leave Raiatea, two men, Dr. Daniel Tyerman and George Bennet, arrived aboard the *Tusan*. They were both members of the LMS board in London and had come on a two-year tour of the Pacific islands to gather information for the London Missionary Society on the progress of their missionaries in the region. John gave them a warm welcome. "At last," he told Mary, "someone from London will understand why we need a ship!"

On November 3, 1821, the *Westmoreland* lay at anchor in the bay beside the Williamses' island home. The ship was on its way from London to Sydney, and the captain agreed to take John and Mary Williams and four-year-old John Jr. aboard. The local Christians were upset to think that John was leaving.

"At present," Tamatoa told John and Lancelot, "we are like a house supported by two strong middle posts; and if one of them is taken away, the house will become weak and will be shaken about by strong winds."

John knew that what Tamatoa was saying was probably true, but he also knew that if the Raiatean church was to become strong, it would have to learn to look to its own local leaders.

As the Williamses prepared to leave, two more men, Papeiha and Vahapata, volunteered to go partway on the journey with John and Mary and be dropped off at Aitutaki, an island located to the west in the Cook Islands. There they would start a missionary work. The thought that they were taking with them local missionaries whom they had trained made it a little easier for John and Mary to leave the people of Raiatea behind.

After several days of sailing, the *Westmoreland* dropped anchor off the island of Aitutaki. Unlike Raiatea, this island was flat and stretched along the top of the reef, enclosing a vast lagoon. The highest point on the island was only a few feet above sea level. Within minutes of arriving, the ship was surrounded by canoes filled with local Polynesians. Many in the canoes had tattoos all over their bodies, others were painted with pipe-clay and red and yellow ochre, and still others had charcoal smeared all over them. And the noise they made was deafening. They chanted, yelled, and let out bloodcurdling screams.

Once John had established who the chief was, he invited him aboard. Although the people of Aitutaki did not speak Tahitian, the language they spoke was close enough for John to make himself understood. He told the chief about how the old gods in Raiatea had been destroyed and in their place the islanders now worshiped the true God. He then introduced Papeiha and Vahapata and told the chief that they had come to tell his people about this new God. The chief was very impressed by what John said and agreed that Papeiha and Vahapata could come ashore and live on Aitutaki, where he promised to watch over them.

John watched as the two Raiateans clambered over the side of the ship and climbed into the chief's canoe. He hoped and prayed that they would experience the same success as the Raiatean missionaries who had gone to Rurutu. And one day, if all went well getting his ailment treated, he would return to Aitutaki and use the island as a jumping-off point to reach Rarotonga with the gospel.

Chapter 7

# The Endeavour

John stood on the deck of the *Westmoreland* as it sailed into Sydney Harbor. It had been more than four years since he was last there, and he was surprised at how much the town had grown.

The Reverend Samuel Marsden welcomed John and Mary back to Sydney. John then settled his wife and son into an LMS guesthouse and set about finding a doctor to treat his swollen legs.

Even before he found a doctor, John noticed that the change of air in Sydney was causing the uncomfortable swelling to go down. Finally he found a doctor who knew what to do. The doctor poked and prodded his inflamed legs and announced that he needed to have the excess fluid drained out of them. After the doctor performed this procedure,

John's health began to improve dramatically, so much so that he no longer worried that his missionary career might be over and that he would need to return to England.

As his health improved, John began to think about going back to Raiatea and picking up his ministry. He also began thinking about things that would aid him in that ministry. And as he thought about it, one thing kept coming to mind—a ship!

John had several reasons for thinking that a ship was a good idea. The two members of the LMS board who had arrived to visit Raiatea just before he left told how the society wanted to encourage the local populations to grow cash crops. This could only mean that the mission society was leaning toward becoming involved in trading, and John felt sure that this time it would understand the need for the missionaries to own their own ship. There were obvious practical advantages to owning a ship rather than hiring one. Owning a ship meant that it would be at the missionaries' disposal to take produce to Sydney at short notice, and it would save the cost of hiring a vessel. A ship would also provide John and the Christians on Raiatea with the ability to send missionaries to many islands.

There was another advantage to owning their own ship. Most of the ships, especially the whaling ships that visited the islands, caused chaos among the local people. The crews brought rum and whiskey to trade for women. They also brought muskets and diseases. The Polynesian Christians did not like it when hoards of sailors came ashore. But as long as they were dependent on hired ships to transport their goods, they had to accept the mayhem the sailors who manned those ships brought to their islands. If the missionaries had their own ship, there would be no need for other ships to put in at these islands.

Shortly before he left Raiatea, John received word that his mother had died. When he got to Sydney, a letter was waiting, informing him that he had received an inheritance from his mother's estate. John decided to use this money to buy a ship. He set out to see what vessels were for sale in Sydney. There were few suitable ships available, but eventually he found a ninety-ton schooner named the *Endeavour*. He would have preferred something larger, but it was the largest of the vessels available, and John decided to pursue purchasing it.

The most delicate part of buying the ship was convincing Samuel Marsden to use London Missionary Society funds to pay for half of it. Because the money from John's inheritance was enough to cover half the purchase price, John needed the mission to put up the rest of the money. At first Samuel would have nothing to do with the plan. He explained to John that the LMS was not in favor of missionaries or churches owning their own ships. However, as the weeks went by, John took every opportunity to point out the value of such a ship. Eventually Samuel relented and agreed to put up half the money.

John immediately purchased the ship and then sat down to write a letter of explanation to the board of the LMS in London. He wrote: "But we must branch out to the right and to the left; for how can we, in justice to the heathen world, especially to the surrounding islands, confine the labours of so many missionaries to so few people."

Now that John had a ship, it was time for him to think about what would be the best crops to transport in it. After talking to many sailors in Sydney, he determined that sugar and tobacco would be good for the islanders to produce. Both sugar cane and tobacco should grow easily in the Society Islands, and they both fetched excellent prices in Europe. With this in mind, John hired Andrew Scott, a young man with experience in overseeing the planting and harvesting of these two crops. He agreed to pay Andrew a salary of 150 pounds a year for three years. It was a lot of money, but if Andrew could teach the islanders to grow sugar cane and tobacco, John considered that he would be worth every penny of his salary.

By April 1822, the *Endeavour* was ready to set sail. On board were supplies of cloth and kettles for the islanders, flour and tea for the missionaries, and several cows and some sheep. The animals were a gift from Sir Thomas Brisbane, the new governor of New South Wales. John was anxious to see whether the animals would adapt to the tropical environment as well as goats had. Sir Thomas also sent along two huge chapel bells and two flags. The flags, one the Union Jack and the other a missionary flag with a white dove on a purple background, were put to immediate use. They waved proudly as the *Endeavour,* under the command of Captain Henry, whom John had hired to run the ship, sailed out of the harbor and into the blue Pacific.

John was pleased with the way his new ship handled, and when they made a stop in the Bay of Islands, little needed to be done to the ship but to make a few adjustments to the rigging. However, while they were stopped there, the wind dropped, and they were forced to stay at anchor for several days. Samuel Marsden had warned John that it was unsafe to set foot in New Zealand at present because a brutal war was going on between the various Maori tribes. John's curiosity got the better of him, though, and he went ashore anyway. What he saw there horrified even a seasoned Pacific traveler like him. One Maori chief cheerfully showed him his newest "prize" possession: the severed head of an opposing chief named Henakee. The chief then described how he had come to get the head. In a letter John relayed the story to his sister in England.

> It is said that he [Henakee] received four [musket] balls before he fell, and that he had no sooner fallen than Shungee...and another chief, called King George, ran up to him, severed his head from his body, and with revengeful glee, caught and drank his blood! O! How horrible! Lord! What is a man that

> thou art mindful of him? But not satiated with his death and his blood, these dreadful monsters cut him in pieces, roasted his flesh, and devoured it as a most delicious meal. The large canoes are now returning from the war, some of them with human heads fixed at the head and stern.

Everyone on board the *Endeavour* was relieved when a wind finally sprang up and filled the sails, allowing the ship to leave New Zealand before too many of the Maori war canoes appeared in the bay.

John had planned on calling into several islands on the way back to Raiatea, but the layover in New Zealand had cost him precious time, and he had to get back before the trade winds died down.

On June 6, six weeks after setting out from Sydney, Captain Henry navigated the *Endeavour* through the reef and into the harbor at Raiatea. Shouts of delight could be heard as the locals recognized John, Mary, and John Jr. standing on the aft deck. Some of the children swam out to the ship while men jumped into their canoes and paddled out to help them ashore.

That night John held a meeting in the chapel and told everyone about the ship and the things he had seen and done while he was away. In return the locals and Lancelot updated John on events on the island in his absence. Most importantly, John wanted to hear news from Aitutaki. He was not disappointed. Two other Raiatean Christians had visited Papeiha and Vahapata and had returned with good news. At first Papeiha and Vahapata were not welcomed on the island. The people of Aitutaki described them as "two logs of driftwood, washed on shore by the waves of the ocean." They had little time for the missionaries' strange message. But the missionaries did not give up. They continued visiting homes on the island and talking to anyone who would listen. Sometimes they were beaten or robbed and were even delivered to the *marae* with a promise that they would be cooked and eaten if they did not leave.

Then a breakthrough occurred. The chief's father was a strong believer in the island's gods. When his daughter became ill, he made all of the right sacrifices and waited for the gods to cure her. When she died, the old man began to think about why he worshiped idols with ears that could not hear and eyes that could not see. He invited Papeiha and Vahapata to talk with him, and as a result he became convinced that their message was true. He ordered his son to destroy all of the *maraes* on the island. Hundreds of others began to listen to the two Raiatean men, and soon their hut was piled with discarded idols as people embraced the gospel.

John was overjoyed. His plan had worked better than he had hoped. Instead of white people trying to explain the gospel to Polynesians, the Polynesians themselves were doing a much more effective job of passing the good news along to one another.

After hearing about the exciting things happening on Aitutaki, John wanted to visit there right away. However, he realized that his first priority was to help Andrew Scott establish crops of sugar cane and tobacco on the island and then send the *Endeavour* to Sydney loaded with the first harvest.

During this time John settled his young son, John Jr., into the new boarding school run by the LMS on Moorea, where he studied alongside the late King Pomare's son and heir to the Tahitian throne. (John had learned that King Pomare of Tahiti had died during the time he was away.)

Finally, on July 4, 1823, John, six Raiatean men, and Robert Bourne, the missionary who had come to Polynesia from England with John on the *Harriet* and the *Active,* set off for Aitutaki aboard the *Endeavour*. The Raiateans had volunteered to be dropped off at other islands in the Cook group that had not yet heard the gospel. During the five-day voyage to Aitutaki, John wrote instructions for these new missionaries on how to go about their work. "They will watch you with rats' eyes," he wrote, "to find little crooked places in your conduct. Therefore be particularly circumspect in all of your conduct. Beware of showing the least anxiety over their property. Beware of pride of heart: do not at all treat them with contempt, but compassionate them, remembering what hath made you to differ from them." John then addressed their behavior toward one another. "Be one in your words. Be one in your actions. Be one in your hearts. Be not obstinate one with another. If God grants us our desire, you will have to baptize, but do not be hasty. Let a little time elapse, and be diligent in observing.

Do not be in haste to prepare laws. You can make known to the chiefs all that has taken place in our islands, and it is with them to desire and propose them. Everything is food in its season. Children are not fed with hard food."

Finally John told the Raiatean men that no matter what happened to them, they should remember four things. First, the church at Raiatea had chosen them and sent them out. Second, God was leading them to wherever they ended up. Third, Christ Himself promised to be with them to the end. And four, God could transform other islands in just the same way He had transformed their own island.

On July 9 the island of Aitutaki came into view on the horizon. Several hours later John was standing on the beach being enthusiastically welcomed by the local population. Papeiha and Vahapata were there, too, and they escorted John to see the new chapel they had just built. The building was two hundred feet long and had a thatched roof. The walls were plastered the same way John had plastered the walls of his house back on Raiatea. John was amazed at the progress the two Raiatean missionaries had made, and that night more than a thousand people gathered in the chapel for a dedication service to officially open the building.

During the service John described how Christians in England raised money to send people like him and the other LMS missionaries out to preach the gospel. When they heard this, the Christians on Aitutaki lamented to John, "We have no money. How sad it is that we cannot imitate our English brothers in giving."

"You might have no money, but you do have something to buy money with," John responded.

This was a new concept to the islanders, and someone in the congregation asked, "What is it we possess that we can buy money with?"

"Pigs" John replied. "You have many pigs. If every family on the island set aside one pig for 'causing the word of God to grow,' when a ship came, those pigs could be sold for money instead of cloth and axes. You would then have money to use to help spread the word of God."

The crowd seemed delighted by the idea, and the next morning John awoke to the squealing of pigs. He stumbled out of his hut to see what the commotion was. He quickly learned that families up and down the island were cutting a notch in the ear of one of their pigs to denote that the animal had been set aside to sell for money that was to be used to help spread the gospel. John was deeply touched by their earnestness.

John discovered that there were a number of people from Rarotonga among the new Christians on Aitutaki. He told them about his desire to go there and begin evangelizing. The people warned him to be careful. Rarotongans had a reputation for treachery and were not to be trusted. They liked the taste of human flesh and had no fear of guns, attacking directly in the face of gunfire. Recently they had attacked a ship that stopped at the island

and had killed three of the vessel's crew and a woman passenger.

The reports of the treachery and brutality of the people of Rarotonga did not deter John. He continued to talk with the Rarotongan Christians, and eventually it was agreed that several of them, along with Papeiha and two lesser chiefs from Aitutaki, would accompany John to Rarotonga.

As the group leaving for Rarotonga gathered on the beach to be transported out to the *Endeavour*, cries and shrieks and bellows suddenly filled the air. The sounds were unlike anything John had ever heard. A group of women burst onto the beach, their bodies smeared in blood that flowed from cuts and scratches all over their bodies. When John stepped forward to ask them why they had mutilated themselves, they told him it was their way of showing sorrow at saying good-bye to their friends who were accompanying him to Rarotonga. John realized that despite the advance of Christianity in Aitutaki, there was still much to be done in teaching the people how to live as Christians and lay aside many of their old harmful ways.

Once the group had been bid farewell by the people of Aitutaki, they were paddled out to the *Endeavour* and climbed aboard. Soon the sails were billowing in the wind and the ship was headed south in the direction of Rarotonga.

Chapter 8

# Rarotonga at Last

Rarotonga proved difficult to find in the wide blue expanse of the Pacific Ocean. The island was not on any regular shipping routes and so did not appear on the map John had with him. After eight days of searching, they spotted another island, which the Rarotongans aboard ship said they thought was Mangaia.

The reputation of the Mangaians was not much better than that of the Rarotongans, and John urged everyone to be cautious. "We are not going to land," he told them. "Papeiha, take two men with you and paddle toward the shore, but do not land. Urge the chief to come back to the ship with you, and we will talk to him."

Papeiha took the canoe they had brought with them from Aitutaki and did as John suggested. Eventually he managed to coax the chief onto the *Endeavour*. The chief, however, could not relax. As Papeiha and John talked to him, his muscles were taut and his eyes darted around the ship. John could understand this behavior when the chief explained that this was the first ship the island's residents had seen since Captain Cook sailed by on his ship, which was also named the *Endeavour*, over thirty years before.

After a long conversation, the chief agreed that four of the missionaries from the ship, two married couples, could stay on Mangaia and teach the people how to read and write and live at peace with one another. Soon after they arrived on the island, the missionaries found out just how much the people of Mangaia needed the particular message of living in peace with one another. Despite the chief's introduction, the islanders tried to strangle the men and rip the clothes off the women as soon as they landed. The missionaries, however, managed to break free and escape to the ship.

Back on the ship everyone agreed it was too dangerous to try to go ashore again, so the *Endeavour* weighed anchor and sailed away. However, John determined to send two single men back to Mangaia in a few months. Perhaps by then the people might be willing to listen to what they had to say.

The next island to appear on the horizon was Atiu, where three months before two native missionaries from Moorea had been sent to share the gospel message. Things had not gone well for them. They were half-starved and stripped of all their belongings, including the booklets containing portions of the Gospels in Tahitian they had brought with them.

As the ship dropped anchor off the island, a large double canoe made its way out from shore. On board was the chief of the island, Roma-Tane. He was a tall, slender man with long, wavy black hair and was dressed in a white shirt and a length of brightly patterned fabric wrapped around his waist. This was known as a *lava-lava* and was worn by many of the Polynesian men.

Roma-Tane climbed aboard the ship, where John and the Polynesian missionaries aboard warmly welcomed him. One of the chiefs from Aitutaki then took Roma-Tane aside and began to talk to him about the Christian God. "We have demolished the *maraes* on our island and burned the great idols. The small idols from our island are in the hold of this ship. They are being taken to Raiatea, the home of the teachers who came to Aitutaki. There the people will see for themselves that the people of Aitutaki have indeed left their old ways and their old gods and embraced the Christian God and His Son, Jesus Christ."

Upon hearing this, Roma-Tane looked surprised. The chief from Aitutaki led him belowdecks to the hold to see for himself the old idols. Holding one of them up, the Aitutakian said, "See, it is made of wood. From a tree we carved this god, and from the same tree we made fire to cook food and eat. Why is it then that we say this idol carved by human hands is more powerful than the wood burned to cook food?"

Roma-Tane's face lit up. He seemed to grasp what he was being told. The following day he asked to become a Christian.

With the chief aboard, the *Endeavour* sailed to the nearby island of Mitiaro, over which Roma-Tane also ruled. There Roma-Tane exhorted the people to tear down their *maraes,* destroy their idols, and listen to what the missionaries they would be leaving on their island said to them.

From Mitiaro they sailed on to Mauke, where Roma-Tane told the people the same thing. As he set foot on the beach, he said, "I am come to advise you to receive the word of Jehovah, the true God, and to leave with you a teacher and his wife, who will instruct you. Let us destroy our *maraes* and burn all the evil spirits with fire. Never let us worship them again. They are wood, which we have carved and decorated and called gods. Here is a teacher to instruct you in the word of the true God. The true God is Jehovah, and the true sacrifice is His Son, Jesus Christ."

After Mauke they returned Roma-Tane to Atiu, where John presented the chief with an axe so that he could cut down trees to make posts for a "house of God."

Before they left Atiu, John asked Roma-Tane whether he had ever heard of Rarotonga. "Oh yes," the chief replied. "It is just one day and one night's sail from Atiu. Wait until the stars shine, and I will show you which way to go."

The following morning the *Endeavour* set sail in the direction that Roma-Tane had indicated. Everyone aboard was feeling jubilant over all that had happened in just a few days on Atiu and the other two islands.

Even with Roma-Tane's directions, Rarotonga did not appear on the horizon. The *Endeavour* battled contrary winds for five days, until nearly all the ship's provisions were used up. Glumly John spoke to all on board at dinner one night. "We will have to give up our hunt for the island if we do not spot it by eight o'clock tonight."

Everyone stayed on deck, squinting their eyes into the setting sun in an attempt to catch a glimpse of a mountain peak jutting from the ocean.

At seven-thirty John had all but given up hope of finding the island. He asked one of the Polynesian men to climb the mast for one last search of the horizon. *"Teie, teie, taua fenua, nei!"* the man yelled excitedly a few minutes later.

"Thank God!" John called back. The island had been spotted.

The following morning Captain Henry cautiously navigated the *Endeavour* toward the reef. Finding no obvious passage through it, he brought the ship to a halt about three miles off the coast and announced that that was as close to the island as it was safe to take the vessel. The canoe was lowered over the side of the ship into the ocean, and Papeiha, Vahineino, and one of the Rarotongan women on board volunteered to go ashore.

Everyone on board the *Endeavour* prayed hard as the two missionaries climbed into the canoe and paddled toward the island. No one on the ship could see what happened once they reached the shore. After two long hours, Papeiha and Vahineino returned, bringing with them a tall young man tattooed from his shoulders to his feet in swirling lines.

"This is Makea, chief of Rarotonga," Papeiha announced.

John stepped forward, and he and Makea rubbed noses, the traditional Polynesian greeting.

The ship then came alive as Makea recognized various Rarotongans on board, including his cousin Tapairu. "You are alive!" he shouted. "We thought the waters had swallowed you up!"

While this was going on, John and Papeiha talked quietly.

"An amazing thing has happened here already," Papeiha told John. "When I told Makea that I was here to tell him about our powerful God and His Son, Jesus Christ, he said, 'We already know about Jesus Christ. A canoe was blown off course and landed on our island. In it was a Tahitian woman, and she told us many things. She said there were white people in the world and that she had met one called Captain Cook, and that after he visited, the servants of another God came to the island. She said this God was a very powerful God—much more powerful than our gods—and that His name was Jehovah and His Son was Jesus Christ. I named two of my sons those names so that I would not forget them, and we made an altar to this big God. Many of our people pray to it, and they come from other islands too because Jehovah is the healer of our diseases.'"

For once John could not think of anything to say! It amazed him to see the way the gospel had spread out ahead of them.

All did not go well for the missionaries in Rarotonga, however. Chief Makea may have named two of his sons Jehovah and Jesus Christ, but he understood little about Christianity. That evening he invited the Rarotongans on board ship to bring their friends and come ashore. He assured them they would be welcome to teach the people about the ways of Jehovah. John and the other Europeans stayed on the ship, not wanting their "strange" appearance to distract the islanders from hearing the gospel.

The Polynesian missionaries were back on board the *Endeavour* as soon as the sun rose the following morning. They had a sad tale to tell. It was almost identical to the problems they had encountered on Mangaia. The Rarotongan men had attacked the missionaries' wives, trying to drag them off into the bushes. The women's tattered clothes told the story.

"What can we do?" John asked the group. He had been certain in his heart that Rarotonga was the key to spreading the gospel throughout the Cook

Islands, and now that dream was looking impossible to realize.

Everyone stood silently for a while, and then Papeiha spoke. "It is not good for the men to stay without their wives, and it is too dangerous for the women to stay. But I have no wife, so I will stay and urge Makea to give up his idols and turn to the one true God."

"Are you sure?" John asked, touched but not surprised by the bravery of his Raiatean Christian brother.

"I am sure," Papeiha replied. "When you return to Raiatea, urge Tiberio to join me, and we shall trust ourselves to the will of God in this place."

That afternoon Papeiha and one of the ship's cats he had befriended paddled ashore again. Papeiha had a woven coconut-frond bag with him containing a spare *lava-lava,* a copy of the New Testament, and five Tahitian grammar books. He turned and waved to John. *"Ko Jehova toku tiaki! Tei roto au i tona rima!"* ("Jehovah is my shepherd! I am in His hand!")

John's eyes filled with tears. He wondered whether he would ever see his brave friend again. Would the people of Rarotonga tire of his teachings and eat him? All John could do was pray for Papeiha and hope for the best as the *Endeavour* sailed back to Raiatea. As they approached the harbor there, those on board hung the idols they had collected from Aitutaki on the yardarms of the ship. This announced to all of the Christians on shore that their mission had met with success.

At home a letter was waiting for John. It was from the board of directors of LMS in response to the news that he had bought the *Endeavour* in Sydney. John read it through quickly; the message was unmistakably plain. The board did not approve of his buying the ship, and he must sell it immediately.

John's heart sank. Would the board ever understand the challenges that their missionaries faced in the Pacific? He doubted they would and knew he had to sell the ship as instructed, though not without a few strong words back to the LMS board.

> Satan knows well that this ship was the most fatal weapon ever formed against his interests in the great South Seas; and therefore, as soon as he felt the effects of its first blow, he wrestled it from out of our hands...I am decidedly of the opinion that a vessel is still wanted in the Islands. A missionary was never designed by Jesus to get a congregation of a hundred or two natives and sit down at his ease as contented as if every sinner was converted, while thousands around him are eating each other's flesh and drinking each other's blood with a savage delight.... For my own part I cannot content myself within the narrow limits of a single reef and if means are not afforded, a continent to me would be infinitely preferable, for there if you cannot ride you walk.

Reluctantly, John supervised the loading of the *Endeavour* with coconut oil and sugar cane for the ship's final voyage to Sydney. It was a sad day as he watched the vessel sail from sight over the horizon. On its way, the *Endeavour* would drop off Tiberio in Rarotonga as Papeiha had requested.

John continued to work with the church at Raiatea, always on the lookout for an opportunity to visit islands that had not yet heard the gospel. There were now nine hundred committed Christians in the church, with more joining every week, giving the church leaders plenty to do.

In March 1824, seven months after John had returned from Rarotonga, Lancelot Threlkeld's wife, Martha, became ill, and within a week she was dead. Soon afterward Lancelot decided to take his four children back to England. It was devastating news to John. He and Lancelot had become very close friends, and John relied on his co-worker for a great deal of advice. John sent a letter back to England with Lancelot, asking the London Missionary Society to appoint another man of equal ability to come and work with him.

Chapter 9

# Messenger of Peace

In November 1825 the Reverend Charles Pitman and his wife, Elizabeth, stepped off a boat in Raiatea. John and Mary Williams welcomed them into their home as guests until a suitable ship arrived to transport them to Rarotonga, where the LMS had commissioned them to work with Papeiha and Tiberio.

As John waited for a ship to arrive, his level of frustration grew. The *Endeavour* would easily have done the job of transporting the Pitmans to Rarotonga, but the LMS board had insisted it be sold. So now they all sat and waited for a ship to arrive. Still, John made the most of the time he had with the Pitmans. He helped them learn the language and showed them how to teach Polynesians to read.

Four months after the Pitmans arrived, Mary discovered she was expecting another baby. The previous three children she had given birth to had all died, and so it was with great joy that the couple welcomed a little boy into the world on November 28, 1826. They named him Samuel Tamatoa Williams after the chief of Raiatea.

At last, in April 1827, a suitable ship dropped anchor in the harbor at Raiatea, and the Pitmans packed up their belongings. By now John was more than ready for another adventure, so he persuaded Mary to bring the new baby and join him on a short trip to Rarotonga. He had heard several reports from passing whaling vessels that the missionary work there was going well, and he also had a letter from Papeiha asking him to visit because the work was "so heavy that they could not carry it alone."

The Pitmans and the Williamses left Raiatea on Sunday, April 25, amid the prayers and good wishes of hundreds of Raiatean Christians who lined the shores. They would need those prayers sooner than they thought. Ominous black clouds gathered on the horizon, and soon the small ship was being relentlessly buffeted about amid the towering waves.

Finally, on Sunday, May 6, the ship arrived off Rarotonga and dropped anchor. The ship's longboat was lowered over the side, and John and Mary and the Pitmans climbed in. Mary clutched baby Samuel as the men rowed the boat ashore. Unfortunately the longboat proved to be less than seaworthy.

Water began pouring in between the hull planks. To stop the boat from sinking, Mary had to sit in the bottom of it, balance the baby on her knee, and frantically bail water. While she did so, John and Charles rowed as hard as they could. Eventually, after a few tense moments, especially when some waves broke around the boat as it passed the reef, they made it ashore. Everyone breathed a prayer of thanks.

Having had to content himself with studying the peaked mountains and lush vegetation of the island from the ship on his previous voyage, John was finally standing on Rarotonga. The first thing he noticed was that, unlike most of the other Pacific islands he had visited, there were no coconut trees. He later learned that a raiding party from another island had attacked Rarotonga two years before and cut down all the coconut palms to punish the locals. The other thing that John noticed about Rarotonga was the rats. They were everywhere. They had arrived on the island on whaling ships, and with no natural predators, they soon overran the place.

When the Williamses and Pitmans arrived, the morning service at the church that Papeiha and Tiberio had built was just finishing. Soon people streamed out to greet John. The people had heard much about him from the two Raiatean missionaries, who also warmly greeted him.

After a feast with Papeiha and Tiberio and the members of the church, the missionaries' baggage was brought ashore from the ship. John and Mary and baby Samuel were given a hut, or *fale,* to live in, and the Pitmans moved into the next-door *fale.*

A few days after they had arrived, Papeiha came to John and Mary. "The people want you to sit outside your door. They have something to show you."

John and Mary sat and waited, and soon they heard Rarotongans singing in the distance. Slowly the singing grew louder until a large crowd of people came into view making their way along a bushy path that led from the interior of the island. The people carried with them huge carvings, some as long as fifteen feet. One by one, the carvings were placed in a pile at John's feet. John counted fourteen of them. One of the elders in the group stepped forward and said, "These were the things we worshiped before the 'Godmen' taught us the right way to go. Now we do not need them anymore, and we ask you: What should we do with them?"

John looked over the pile of idols, imagining how much suffering their worship had caused—the babies sacrificed and eaten, the old men and women killed and their blood sprinkled at the base of these idols. Now the Word of God had changed the hearts of many Rarotongan people, and for that John was grateful. "Let us set the longest idols aside and use them as the upright poles for our new chapel," he said. "That way, when you stand in church, you will remember what the true God has delivered you from."

The people all agreed that that would be a good end for their idols. The following day John set about supervising the building of a new chapel. Now that over four thousand people were gathering for church each Sunday, the existing building Papeiha and Tiberio had built was too small.

One morning soon afterward, John was reminded just how isolated the Rarotongan people had been up until now. He was working on the foundations of the new chapel when he realized he had left his set-square in his hut. He had no paper with him, so he picked up a chip of wood and wrote on it, "Mary, please send my set-square." He then called over one of the workmen, a Rarotongan who did not go to church. "Friend, take this to my house and give it to Mrs. Williams," he instructed.

The man gave John a puzzled look and then blurted out, "Take that! She will call me a fool and scold me if I carry a chip of wood to her."

"No," John replied. "She will not scold you. Take it and run fast. I am in a hurry."

The man took the chip from John. "But what should I say?" he asked.

"You don't have to say anything. The chip will say all I wish," John said.

The man held up the chip of wood and laughed. "How can this speak? Has this a mouth?"

"No, but Mrs. Williams will know what it says. Go and show it to her. You will see."

The man went running off and returned several minutes later. John heard him yelling before he arrived. "See the wisdom of the English people. They can make chips talk, they can make chips talk!" The man held the chip high in one hand and the set-square in the other. As he handed John the set-square he said, "Can I keep this chip which talks?"

John smiled in agreement, and the man poked a hole in it and strung it around his neck. For several days after that, John often saw small groups of people standing around the man as he expounded on the wonders of the talking chip.

The man's unfamiliarity with writing got John thinking about why Papeiha and Tiberio were not having much success in teaching the Rarotongans to read. As soon as the new church was completed, he turned his attention to education. He noticed that Rarotongan was quite different from the Tahitian dialect of the Polynesian language. John set about mastering the new dialect. As soon as he felt confident that he was using the correct Rarotongan words, he began translating into Rarotongan the Gospel of John and the letter to the Galatians, along with some simple reading books. He hoped that having these in the Rarotongan dialect would make the process of learning to read easier, especially since Papeiha and Tiberio were still using the Tahitian grammar books they had brought with them as the basis for their teaching.

The Rarotongans were very excited when John announced "Rat Extermination Day." The rats were such a problem on the island that everyone had a tale to tell about them. For instance, Elizabeth

Pitman told John that one night she had left her leather shoes beside the bed, only to be awakened by a strange noise. She peered over the edge of the bed and saw a huge rat dragging her shoes away. In the morning she found only the soles of the shoes outside in the sand.

On the appointed day, every man, woman, and child on the island was armed with a stick and told to go out and club the rats in the village. Thirty large woven baskets about six feet long were placed at collection points, and then the hunt began. In less than an hour all thirty baskets were filled to overflowing with dead rats, and still hundreds more rats were scampering away into the bush for their lives. John could see that they would have to think of another way to get rid of the vermin.

Soon after this Chief Makea, several of the island's elders, and the missionaries got together to make new laws for Rarotonga. Until now such laws had been impossible. No one had thought that various groups on the island could or would live together in peace. Even the treatment of family members was often harsh. The Rarotongans had a custom called *Ao Anga.* Papeiha explained to John that *Ao Anga* meant that when a man died, his brothers swarmed his house and took everything he owned away—clothes, mats, and food. They left nothing for the man's widow or his children. As a result, many times the widow and children starved to death. No one seemed to care. But now that the missionaries had come to the island, the people wanted laws that protected the weak and the young. After much talking, many of the laws put in place on Raiatea were adopted in Rarotonga.

Each Sunday more people were at church than the previous week. This encouraged John greatly, though he found out that not all of the preaching was going on within the confines of a building. He had often passed Buteve's house and greatly admired his well-kept garden. This was no small feat for Buteve because both his arms and his legs had been withered away by disease. Still, he used the stumps of his arms to position a stick in the ground and then threw his full weight on it, loosening the soil so that he could plant seeds. One evening as John walked by, Buteve shouted, "Welcome, servant of God, who bought light into this dark island!"

John stopped to talk with Buteve, and he was astonished at how much the man knew about the Bible, especially since he had never seen Buteve in church. "Where did you obtain your knowledge?" he asked.

"From you, to be sure. Who brought us news of salvation but you and those you sent ahead?"

"That's true," John replied, "but I do not recollect ever seeing you come to hear me speak of these things, so how do you understand them?"

"Why," Buteve replied, a glint in his eye, "as the people return from services, I take my seat by the wayside and beg for a bit of the Word from them as they pass by. One gives me one piece, someone else another piece, and I collect them together in my heart. By thinking over what I have been given and praying to God to make it known to me, I understand a little about His Word."

John was astonished and delighted to hear this, and from then on, whenever he passed Buteve's house, he stopped in for an interesting conversation.

Things continued to go well on Rarotonga, and after eight months John was satisfied that the Pitmans had adjusted to life on the island. It was now time to think about returning to Raiatea. This proved difficult, however. Not a single ship had passed the island since John and Mary had arrived, and John began to wonder whether he might be stranded there for years. Once again his thoughts turned toward owning a ship in which to get around the islands. This time, though, there were no ships to buy. If he wanted a ship to get off Rarotonga, he would have to build one. And that is what John decided to do.

Before he started building the ship, John took stock of the tools he had to work with. He had a pickax, a hoe, an adze, several hatchets, and several hammers. As well, he had a length of heavy iron chain that had been abandoned on the beach by a whaling ship three years before. John decided that he would use this to fashion the metal fittings necessary for the ship.

Before he could mold and shape the metal chain, John had to build a forge. And before he could build a forge, he needed to make some bellows to pump air to the fire to get it hot enough. For this purpose three of the four goats on the island were killed, and their hides were to be used in place of leather for the bellows. However, before John could finish his forge, the rats had eaten the goatskins. John then made a bellows from a box with two chambers in it and a pistonlike device that sucked air into the box and then blew it out into the fire. Once the forge was built, John used charcoal instead of coal as fuel for the fire and got busy. The locals lined up to crank the bellows and watch John work. John used a large rock as an anvil and began heating and reshaping the links of the chain. The Rarotongan men were amazed at what he did with the metal. "Why didn't we think of heating the hard stuff instead of just trying to beat it with stones to change its shape?" they exclaimed to one another.

John then set to work on the hull. With no saw, the trees were cut down with a hatchet and the logs split using wedges. The planks were then smoothed with the adze and two of the hatchets with long crooked handles tied to them. Slowly the hull began to take shape. There was not enough iron to make metal spikes to hold the ship together, so holes were bored in the roughhewn planks and wooden pegs were driven through the holes and into the frame beneath to hold the vessel together.

Of course there was no way of steaming the planks so that they could be bent and molded to the curve of the hull. When John wanted planks of a particular shape, he bent a piece of bamboo to the shape he wanted and sent some of the men out to find a tree growing in that shape. When they found such a tree they cut it down and split it, thus providing two or three planks that shape.

Once the hull, which was about sixty feet long and eighteen feet wide, was built, coconut husks, the dried stalks of bananas, and pieces of native cloth, or *tapa,* were used instead of oakum to caulk the seams between the planks and make the ship watertight.

After the hull was caulked and the two masts were in place, it was time to think about sails and rigging. The sails were made from local woven sleeping mats that were quilted to give them more strength against the wind. The ropes for the rigging were made from strips of bark from the hibiscus tree. John made a crude machine for twisting the strips of bark together to form rope.

The next challenge for John was to make the wheels for the blocks used to raise and furl the sails. Because the wheels had to be perfectly round, he made a lathe to turn them. Using wood from the ironwood tree, he began producing the necessary wheels. One of the local chiefs was so taken with John's efforts on the lathe that he took the first piece produced, threaded a strip of hide through it, and proceeded to wear it around his neck. He pranced up and down through the village showing off his new adornment. The people both admired it and were astonished at how it had been made. "If we had not given up our idols, surely this would have been worshiped and given precedence over all our other idols," said one man when he saw the piece of turning handiwork.

Finally the boat, which John had christened the *Messenger of Peace,* was ready to be launched. Once the vessel was finally coaxed into the water, all that was needed was to fit the rudder. Because there was not enough iron left to make pintles to hold the rudder in place, John melted down the pickax, the adze, and the hoe to make them. However, he was worried that they wouldn't be strong enough, so he loaded a substitute rudder aboard the boat in case the first one failed. The *Messenger of Peace,* which had taken three months to build, was now finally ready to set sail.

Since Raiatea was about eight hundred miles away, John thought it would be wise to first try out the *Messenger of Peace* on a shorter voyage. He decided to head for Aitutaki, which was 170 miles north. There he would check up on the church and the missionaries and gather supplies for Rarotonga.

John chose a crew of Rarotongans to man the ship, and with him at the helm, they set sail. Much to John's dismay, six miles out from Rarotonga, the inexperienced crew let the foresail go in a strong wind. With a sickening crack the foremast snapped, and they were forced to turn back and make repairs.

Once a new mast had been installed, the *Messenger of Peace* got under way again. John was pleased with the way the boat handled in the open water, and they arrived at Aitutaki without further incident.

John stayed on Aitutaki for ten days, and when the *Messenger of Peace* left for the return voyage, it was laden with gifts for the people of Rarotonga. The gifts included seventy pigs, thirty cats, many woven baskets and mats, and hundreds of coconuts. The gifts were well received. The cats did kill some rats, but much to John's surprise, the pigs killed a lot more. John hoped it would not be too long before the rat problem was finally under control.

The coconuts were left to sprout and then were planted up and down the beaches to replace the trees that had been destroyed by the raiding party. In a year or so the coconut trees would once again provide food and weaving material for the people of Rarotonga.

On April 1, 1828, a ship was sighted from the beach. A longboat was lowered over the side of the vessel, and John and Mary stood watching with many of their friends to see who would come ashore. Much to their joy it was another missionary couple, named Aaron and Sarah Buzacott, who had been send out by the London Missionary Society to work in Rarotonga. Sarah cradled a month-old baby in her arms. The Buzacotts had brought plenty of supplies with them, including items the missionaries had run out of months ago, such as flour and tea.

That evening, after the formal island welcome was over, the Buzacotts and Pitmans sat with John and Mary in front of their house overlooking the lagoon. John savored his cup of tea. It was the first one he'd had in many months, and to make it even better, he was able to stir some sugar into it. While he enjoyed having tea to drink once again, he knew that Mary was especially grateful for the flour and rice she now had to cook with. They had lived on a diet of mainly breadfruit, fish, and bananas during their time in Rarotonga. Although his wife had tried not to complain, he knew the familiar food was a welcome relief to her, especially since she was expecting another baby in a month or so and was feeling weak and exhausted.

John was delighted to learn that, besides being an ordained minister, Aaron Buzacott was a practical man. Aaron had been raised on a farm in Devon before becoming an ironmonger. And John's eyes lit up when he learned that Aaron had had the foresight to bring a load of iron with him. Aaron and John quickly planned how to use some of it to strengthen the hull of the *Messenger of Peace.*

The Buzacotts also brought news from Raiatea, which they had visited en route to Rarotonga. The news was not good. Tuahine, a very capable deacon who had been left in charge of the church, had died suddenly. This had left a void in the church leadership, and there were many arguments and divisions among the people over who should take his place. And there was more bad news. Two large canoes filled with Raiatean Christians had capsized in a storm. All seventy-six people on board the two canoes had drowned.

All this bad news made John anxious to get back to Raiatea. On April 12 the *Messenger of Peace,* its hull now strengthened with some of the iron Aaron had brought, was ready to set sail. John found it very hard to say good-bye to his many new friends, but he was confident that the Pitmans and the Buzacotts would make excellent missionaries and would be good friends to the Rarotongans.

Several Rarotongans were going along to crew the *Messenger of Peace.* Among them was Chief Makea, who was eager to meet other Christian chiefs from the islands.

On the evening of the ship's departure, several thousand people gathered on the beach to bid the missionaries farewell. As the Williams family was rowed to the *Messenger of Peace,* the people began to sing in beautiful harmony from the shore, *"Kia ora e Tama ma. I te aerenga i te moana e!"*

John translated the words out loud: "Blessings on you, beloved friends. Blessings on you in journeying on the deep!"

His eyes filled with tears as he turned to Mary, who had Samuel cuddled close beside her, and said, "Isn't it amazing what God has accomplished among these people in such a short time?"

Chapter 10

# Questions

The *Messenger of Peace* arrived back in Raiatea on April 27, 1828. The caulking on her sides was hanging off in long strips, and her sails had several holes. Even so, the ship was an instant sensation. Everyone poured onto the beach at Va'oara to welcome the Williams family back and to meet Chief Makea and the Rarotongan crew. A great round of feasting and speechmaking followed over the next several days.

Once things settled down, John's first job was to sort out the problems that had developed in the church while he was away. This did not prove to be too difficult. So much excitement had been generated among the people over the return of their missionary and the many stories he had to tell that those in the church were soon ready to work together again in getting the gospel out to other islands.

When the baby Mary was expecting was stillborn, John decided to stay put for a while in Raiatea and help his wife. He was glad, however, when the *Messenger of Peace* was pressed into service without him on board. After new cloth sails had been fitted and the caulking reapplied, a crew was selected, and two missionaries and several Raiatean Christians journeyed to the Marquesas Islands to set up a mission station.

While they were gone, John set about making a smaller boat to send home Chief Makea and the Rarotongan men who had crewed the *Messenger of Peace* to Raiatea. With them John also sent one of the deacons from the church to help the missionaries in Rarotonga.

As John worked, he dreamed about spreading the gospel to the islands that were thousands of miles to the west of Raiatea. A voyage to these islands would be long and dangerous, and he knew that in the past Mary had objected to the idea of his being away for such long periods of time. Recently, however, she'd had a change of heart. John recalled with great joy her exact words to him. "From this time your desire has my full concurrence; and when you go, I shall follow you every day with my prayers, that God may preserve you from danger, crown your attempt with success, and bring you back in safety."

Now that Mary supported his dream completely, John was free to plan his most ambitious mission trip yet. When the *Messenger of Peace* returned from the Marquesas, he and fellow missionary Charles Barff would take eight Raiatean volunteers and head for the Fiji islands and other islands still farther west.

Finally, on February 25, 1830, the *Messenger of Peace* lay anchored in the bay at Va'oara. John had planned to leave on his voyage as soon as the annual May missionary festival was finished. The festival proved to be an exciting event. Large numbers of Christians from other islands in the Society group, including Borabora, Taha'a, and Huahine, sailed or paddled to Raiatea. Then, two days before the festival was due to begin, the HMS *Seringapatam* dropped anchor off Va'oara. At first John was concerned to see an English ship anchored off the island, mostly because he feared that the riotous behavior of the sailors would disrupt the Christian gathering. He need not have worried. The ship's master, Captain Waldegrave, was a Christian who insisted that his crew remain orderly at all times. In fact, the captain and his officers accepted John's invitation to attend a mission festival service, which began at ten o'clock the following morning. After a brief stop for lunch, the service continued until six in the evening.

John watched the captain closely as the day proceeded. The captain appeared to be stirred when the Polynesians sang the popular hymn "Blow Ye the Trumpet, Blow" in Tahitian. Then the chief of

Taha'a stood and addressed the crowd. "Praise to God well becomes us," he began. "But let it be heart-praise. All the work we do for God must be heart-work....We were dwelling formerly in a dark house, among centipedes and lizards, spiders and rats; nor did we know what evil and despicable things were around us. The lamp of light, the Word of God, has been brought, and now we behold with dismay and disgust these abominable things. But stop. Some are killing each other this very day while we are rejoicing; some are destroying their children while we are saving ours; some are burning themselves in the fire while we are bathing in the cool waters of the gospel. What shall we do? We have been told this day by our missionary that God works by sending His Word and His servants. To effect this, property must be given. We have it; we can give it. Prayer to God is another means: Let us pray fervently. But our prayer will condemn us if we cry, 'Send forth thy word and make it grow,' and do not use the means. I shall say no more but let us cleave to Jesus."

Several other men got up and spoke just as eloquently, and when the service was finished John overheard three officers off the *Seringapatam* talking among themselves.

"It's just not possible," one of them said. "There's no way those chiefs wrote their own speeches."

"I agree," interjected a second officer. "They are just parrots, all of them. They cannot possibly understand what they are saying."

John smiled to himself. He knew it must seem incredible to these officers who plied the Pacific Ocean in their ship. They were used to encountering illiterate, superstitious people, not Polynesians who could read and think for themselves.

The following morning, Captain Waldegrave and the Reverend Watson, the ship's chaplain, knocked at John's door. "I am sorry to bother you," Captain Waldegrave began when John opened it. "I suppose you have heard by now that many of my crew are finding it difficult to believe that the men who spoke yesterday were not coached for our benefit."

John laughed. "Yes, it does seem impossible that these men know what they are talking about, doesn't it? But let me assure you, they do know. If you like, I will prove it to you. Why don't you both have a cup of tea with me, and I will send someone off to find twelve or fifteen of our people. I am sure they will be happy to answer any questions you wish to put to them."

"Would you mind?" the Reverend Watson replied. "I personally am ready to believe them, but many of the others are not, and I think it would do you a great deal of good back in England if the people could demonstrate such an astounding grasp of the Scriptures."

"Of course," John replied, opening the door wide. "Come in and join me for tea. I have nothing to hide."

An hour later fifteen men and women from various islands were assembled on John's veranda. John joined them there with the captain and the chaplain.

"Thank you for coming," he said. "These gentlemen would like to ask you a few questions, which I am sure you can answer with confidence." Then he turned to the two men. "Go ahead, gentlemen, ask away."

"Do you believe that the Bible is the Word of God and that Christianity is of divine origin?" John translated Captain Waldegrave's words into Tahitian.

Once the Polynesian Christians understood what was being asked, they looked at each other with puzzlement on their faces. John knew that the captain might think it was because the question was too difficult for them, but in fact, he knew that it was a question they had never asked themselves before. No Polynesian he had ever spoken to doubted that the Bible was the Word of God.

After a long pause, one of the men replied, "We most certainly do. We look at the power that has caused the overthrow of idolatry among us, and we believe that no human could make us abandon our idols, our gods."

There was a round of head nodding, and then another person spoke up. "I believe the Scriptures to be of divine origin on account of the system of salvation they reveal. We had a religion before, transmitted to us by our ancestors, whom we considered the wisest of men; but how dark and black that system was, compared with the bright scheme of salvation presented in the Bible. Here we learn that we are sinners; that God gave His own Son Jesus Christ to die for us; and that through believing, the salvation He earned became ours. Now, what but the wisdom of God could have devised such a system as this?"

Then an old man who had once been a priest of the god Oro and was now a devout Christian stood. He looked at the captain and the chaplain and then held his hands up high and moved the joints of his wrists and fingers. Then without saying a word he opened and shut his mouth several times. Then he stood on one wobbly leg and raised the other as high as he could and moved it around. Then he spoke. "See, I have hinges all over me; if the thought grows in my heart that I want to carry anything, the hinges in my hands enable me to do so; if I want to utter anything, the hinges of my jaws enable me to say it; and if I desire to go anywhere, there are hinges to my legs to enable me to walk. Now, I perceive great wisdom in the adaptation of my body to the various wants of my mind; and when I look into the Bible and see there proofs of wisdom, which correspond exactly with those that appear in my frame, I conclude that the Maker of my body is the Author of that book."

"Well answered," Captain Waldegrave said as the old man sat back down on the woven mat. "Now I have another question for you. What are the prophets in the Bible?"

Several people jumped up to answer this question. The first person to his feet replied, "They are persons inspired by God to foretell events ages before they occurred."

"Can you name any of them?" the captain asked.

"Yes," came the reply. "There is Samuel, David, Isaiah, Daniel, Jonah, and many others."

"You have mentioned Isaiah. Can you tell me any of his prophecies?" the captain continued.

"Of course. He was the prophet who wrote so much about our Lord and Savior and who said that He should be numbered with the transgressors, and we know that Christ was crucified between two thieves. There was the prophecy and its fulfillment."

The questioning continued, and the Polynesians answered questions on Moses, Jesus, and Christian doctrine. They never faltered in their answers. Finally Captain Waldegrave handed a Tahitian New Testament to one person and asked him to open it at random and read a verse aloud. Then he asked the person a question about the meaning of the verse. Around the veranda the New Testament was passed until every person, even the shyest ones, had read a verse and answered questions on it.

When the two men were finally finished with their questioning, John looked at his watch. Three hours had passed!

As the captain left, he shook John's hand heartily. "Much of the sincerity and piety of the church members in this island has been doubted, but from all that I have observed, I am led to the fervent prayer that I myself might be at last equally worthy with many of these to take my place in heaven."

"Quite right!" the Reverend Watson agreed. "What we have seen here is truly remarkable. You can be sure we will not be silent about it when we return to England."

On May 24, 1830, ten days after the *Seringapatam* had left, John and Charles Barff, along with several Raiatean teachers, set out on the *Messenger of Peace*. Their first port of call was Moorea, to drop off Mary and Samuel. In the hope that her health would improve, Mary had decided to stay with friends in Moorea while John was gone. As well, John Jr. was still on the island, attending the Royal South Seas Academy, as the school on Moorea was now called.

From Moorea John and the others headed westward to Mangaia, where John had sent two single Polynesian missionaries to work several years before. As John and Charles came ashore on Mangaia, about five hundred of the local people were waiting to greet them. "We welcome you as God's men!" they shouted from the beach. "Do you carry the Word of God on chips for us?"

Nothing could have pleased John more than to hear these words from the people. It represented a remarkable change from the previous time he had come to the island. Then the locals had tried to kill the missionary men and assault their wives when they came ashore. John and Charles and the Raiatean teachers stayed safely on the island for a week. During that time they were able to explain to the Christians some of the finer points of the gospel. Given the people's limited understanding of some areas of doctrine, John was not surprised to learn that the first wave of Christian conversions on the island had led to conflict. The Mangaians who continued to practice idol worship had become very angry with those who had given it up, and fighting had broken out. The Christians had won the fight, but not with very Christian conduct! Even though the idol worshipers had begged for mercy, the Christians had hacked them to pieces. By the time John arrived, the fighting had ceased, but the hatred between the two groups ran deep.

To help bridge this gap, John and several of the Raiatean Christians took the step of visiting the idol worshipers and listening to their grievances. By doing this, they were able to convince both sides to make a fresh start, and by the end of their stay on the island, several more converts had joined the church.

From Mangaia it was two days' sailing to Atiu, where a large group had gathered to celebrate the marriage of their chief Roma-Tane to the daughter of a chief from the nearby island of Mauke. The crew of the *Messenger of Peace* joined in the great feast and made many friends among the visitors from Mauke.

That night John and Charles stayed on the island instead of returning to the ship, though they had to take turns sleeping. Throughout the night islanders came to visit them, asking questions about Christianity and begging the missionaries to teach them more hymns.

On the second day at Atiu, the wives of the two Polynesian missionaries serving there pulled John aside. "We are in much distress," they said. "Our husbands have to work very hard fishing all week, and especially on Saturdays so that we can have fish to eat on Sunday. So we are left alone in the village many times. We write on our slates everything that we can remember from the preaching our husbands do, but it not enough to satisfy our neighbors. They come to us every day asking us for God's words, and we have run out of words to tell them!"

"I understand," John replied. "The people here are very eager to learn, aren't they?"

"Yes, but it is easy for you to teach them," one of the women said. "You are like a spring from which knowledge is continually bubbling up. You have nothing to do but open your mouth and out it flows."

John had never thought of himself as a bubbling spring before, but he could see the women's point. They were being asked to assume the role of Christian teachers with no materials to help them. "I will write out some Bible studies for you before I leave," he promised. "And when I get back to Raiatea, I will print some Christian teaching pamphlets and see that they are brought back for you to use."

From Atiu the group traveled on to Mauke and Mitiaro. John was impressed with the work of the two Polynesian missionaries on these islands. For twelve years Laavi on Mauke and Taua on Mitiaro had worked to teach the gospel and establish a church and school. On both islands John found the people living simple, joyful Christian lives.

From Mitiaro the *Messenger of Peace* set sail for Rarotonga. John had told Charles many exciting stories about his stay on Rarotonga, and both men waited expectantly for the island to appear on the horizon. When two and a half days later the *Messenger of Peace* squeezed through the narrow opening in the reef and dropped anchor in the small harbor at Avarua on Rarotonga, John was surprised that there was no welcome for them. A few children were waiting at the water's edge with Aaron Buzacott, his face long and drawn from worry. John wondered what possibly could have gone wrong. Where were the adults, and why weren't they there to meet him?

Chapter 11

# A Change in Plans

Aaron warmly greeted John as he stepped ashore, but he had tears in his eyes.

"What is it?" John asked.

"An epidemic," Aaron replied. "Several months ago a whaling ship stopped in at the island, and soon afterward people began getting sick and dying. The disease has ravaged the island."

The condition of the Rarotongans saddened John. Some of the people looked like walking skeletons. John talked to the people and prayed with them. And all too often when he inquired about a person who had been a friend on his previous stay, the answer was the same: "He is dead."

Sarah Buzacott was finding the situation hard to bear and broke down in tears when John arrived.

John tried to comfort her and her husband as best he could. They had seen too many good people die, and the emotional toll of these deaths weighed heavy on them.

While John traveled on to the other side of the island to visit the Pitmans, Charles Barff returned to the *Messenger of Peace* to fetch some medicine. Back on the island he distributed it to those who were ailing. There was not enough of the medicine for everyone who was sick, but he hoped and prayed that the concoction would help those who did receive it.

With heavy hearts, John and Charles set sail again. Leaving the troubles of Rarotonga behind, they hoped for better news in Aitutaki.

John was relieved to find that the epidemic had not reached Aitutaki. Everyone there was healthy and excited at the arrival of the *Messenger of Peace.* A special meeting of the church was called to welcome John and the other missionaries, and after several hymns had been sung, one of the deacons stood up and made an announcement. "We still remember your words to us many years ago, and we have something to give you." With that he held out a small woven bag. "You told us to set aside a pig to sell and raise money for the work of God. Each year the families of the church have clipped the ear of one of their pigs and set it aside. And each year the money raised for the work of God grows. Not long ago a ship called here, and we asked the captain to buy our pigs. He consented.

This is the money our pigs bought." With that the deacon walked proudly over to John and handed him the bag.

John thanked him and looked inside.

"Count it," the deacon said. "We are happy to dedicate it to Christ."

John stood up and pulled out an assortment of bills. His astonishment grew as he reached 50, then 100, and finally 103 pounds! As he finished counting the money, the entire group, numbering about two thousand, burst into clapping and singing.

It was a wonderful moment for John, who wished that members of the LMS board could have been there to see it. Perhaps then they would understand his passion for ships to aid in spreading the gospel to the other islands of the Pacific.

The next day the Aitutakians were eager to show off their Bible knowledge. Over four hundred children presented themselves to John and Charles for an exam on what they knew. John was amazed at how much they had learned, especially since the only parts of the Bible that they had access to were the Book of Acts and several of the apostle Paul's letters. Even these were not complete, as the Christians had torn the binding off them so that they could share the single pages with one another. Most of what they learned had been recited to them by their Raiatean teachers. But as impressive as their knowledge was, it highlighted the desperate need to print more of the Bible in the various Polynesian dialects.

When it was time for the group to leave Aitutaki, two families and several other single men volunteered to go along as missionary teachers to the Fijians.

Six days of pleasant sailing westward brought them to an island that Captain Cook had called Savage Island (today called Niue). John hoped that the local people had calmed down since Captain Cook's disastrous visit, but he wasn't prepared to take any chances. Once the *Messenger of Peace* lay at anchor off a long, sandy beach on the island, he ordered a man to climb the mast and wave a white flag. In quick response a group of men appeared on the beach and began waving a piece of cloth.

"But they are not getting in their canoes to greet us," John said thoughtfully as he leaned on the railing. "I think it will be safe for us to go to them, as long as there are no white people in the boat to alarm them."

"We will go," said two of the men from Aitutaki.

A canoe was lowered over the side of the ship with the two men in it. John took out his spyglass and watched anxiously as they paddled toward the shore. When they were about two hundred yards off the beach, the men stopped rowing and bowed their heads. John knew they were praying, and when he looked at the Savage Islanders he knew why! By now about fifty big, strong men were gathered on the beach. Each of them carried three or four spears and a slingshot. John swung the spyglass back to the canoe where the two men

were motioning for the islanders to put down their weapons. None of them did.

Finally the boat reached the shore, and the Aitutakian men got out. For a long moment no one moved, and then John watched as one of the islanders stepped forward with a breadfruit and a coconut frond. It was a good sign, an *utu,* or sign of welcome that Polynesians sometimes gave a stranger as a way of saying they would not fight them.

The men talked for a while, and then some of the islanders launched their canoes and followed the two men toward the ship. As they got closer, some of the canoes began lagging behind until only one canoe followed the two Aitutakian men.

John noticed that the man in this canoe was older than most of the others and his hair was decorated with red feathers, which meant he was probably the chief. "Welcome. All is good between us. Come on board," John yelled in Tahitian to him.

The chief stopped paddling, his eyes large with fear. John repeated his invitation several more times, until the chief finally took up his paddle again. Five minutes later the chief was on board, though he did not stop leaping around the deck long enough for John to hold any kind of conversation with him. The more the crew tried to calm him, the more agitated the chief became, gnashing his teeth and frantically waving his arms about. John had to remind himself that most of the items nearby were completely foreign to the chief. He tried to give the chief a hatchet, a knife, scissors, and a mirror, but none of them interested him. Then the chief saw a large mother-of-pearl shell on deck. He dropped the other objects and ran over to it, signaling that this was the prize he really wanted.

Meanwhile the rest of the canoes and the two men from Aitutaki had returned to the beach, where the islanders gestured at them. The chief got back in his canoe, too, and as he paddled ashore, the two teachers pushed their boat into the water and headed back to the ship. "They do not want us!" one of them yelled to John as they got closer. "They told us to leave before they sacrifice us to their gods."

"We will have to leave this in the hands of God," John said, trying not to sound too disappointed. This was the first island he had visited where not one person appeared to welcome them.

John decided to press on westward, but as he did, he began to have second thoughts about his original plan. With his lack of success on Savage Island, he wondered whether going on to the Fiji islands and then, as he had hoped, to the New Hebrides was such a good idea. He had heard that some veteran Wesleyan missionaries were working in the Tongan Islands to the southwest, and he thought it might be wise to visit them first before going any farther west. Perhaps these missionaries would have information and insights that would help him in his mission. So the *Messenger of Peace* changed course and headed for Tongatapu, the main island in the Tonga group, about 350 miles away.

John had heard a lot about Tongatapu over the years. Ten London Missionary Society missionaries from the original group sent out from England on the *Duff* had first set foot on the island in 1797, a year after John was born. But they encountered many problems, and within two years they were all gone. Three of the missionaries were caught in the middle of a local fight and killed, six others fled for their lives, and one chose to give up his Christian beliefs and live among the islanders.

No more attempts were made by European missionaries to work in the Tongan islands until the Wesleyans sent in two men, John Thomas and John Hutchinson, in 1826. The two men were followed a year later by two more men, Nathaniel Turner and William Cross. Amazingly, when John Thomas and John Hutchinson arrived on the island of Tongatapu they found in the village of Nuku'alofa a Christian church and school. Three Tahitian missionaries had gone to the Tongan Islands in the early 1820s. They eventually settled on Tongatapu and worked diligently teaching the gospel there. Surprised and delighted to find Christians already among the Tongan people, the Wesleyan missionaries took over running the church, and the last of the Tahitian teachers returned home in 1828.

On Thursday, June 25, 1830, the *Messenger of Peace* sailed past the mountainous island of Eua and then on to Tongatapu, a long, low island surrounded by a reef and several smaller islands. Gingerly they navigated their way through a maze of reefs, shoals, and rocky outcrops until they were safely at anchor off Nuku'alofa. Much to their surprise, another schooner was anchored off the village.

John and Charles rowed ashore and were greeted by Nathaniel, who welcomed them warmly. Soon they were enjoying a meal with Nathaniel and William and their wives and children. John was delighted to hear about the progress these Wesleyan missionaries were making and the news that John Thomas had settled in one of the northern islands of the Tonga group.

Finally John's curiosity got the better of him. "Who does the schooner anchored off the village belong to?" he asked.

"A Christian trader by the name of Samuel Henry. You might have heard of him. His father was an LMS missionary who came out on the *Duff* and settled in Tahiti. A wonderful man he is," Nathaniel replied.

"What is he doing here?" John continued. "Do you send crops to Sydney with him?"

"Sometimes, but that is not the reason he is here. He brought a chief from Fiji with him. His name is Takai, and he came to ask us to send teachers to spread the gospel in his island. He is very persistent, and we don't know what to tell him. The only Polynesian I would feel comfortable sending at present is a man named Fauea. But sending him creates a whole new problem."

"How so?" John asked, sipping the wonderful cup of tea Jane Cross had just served him.

"Strangely enough, Fauea is not from here. He is a Samoan who has been living on Tongatapu for eighteen years. He has a Tongan wife and many children, and they are all Christians. Recently he has been telling me he wants to take the gospel back to Samoa, but we Wesleyans are not intending to spread ourselves in that direction just yet."

John's mind whirled with possibilities, but it was not until after he had met Fauea that he decided to present his plan to Nathaniel and William. One evening after dinner, John and Charles and the two Wesleyan missionaries sat together under a large mango tree.

"We need to plan ahead," John began. "Right now many islands are opening up, and the biggest waste of our resources would be to both go after the same island while leaving another untouched. We all know that the LMS and the Wesleyans have always worked side by side in the Pacific, so let us work out a way to get the gospel to every island as smoothly as possible."

"Here, here," William responded. "Besides, two different missionary groups working in one area would confuse the islanders. I'd hate to see them torn apart by small matters of doctrine after they have been saved from idol worship and eating each other!"

The conversation and planning continued for several days and grew to include the Fijian Takai, the Samoan Fauea, and the Polynesian missionaries from the *Messenger of Peace*. The results made John very happy, although it meant he had to change his plans. The missionaries, realizing there was plenty of work for all of them, decided to divide up the western islands of Polynesia. They agreed that the Wesleyans should continue their efforts in Tonga and spread their work into Fiji while the LMS should keep working in the Society Islands and move into the Samoan islands. This still left the problem of a lack of teachers to go back to Fiji with Takai, and for Fauea, who wanted to return to Samoa. The solution was for the Polynesian missionaries to swap missions so that Fauea would go to Samoa with John and Charles under LMS leadership. Meanwhile, a number of the Raiateans and Aitutakians traveling with John would go to Fiji with Takai aboard Samuel Henry's schooner and come under the leadership of the Wesleyans.

Together they also decided to stay away from the New Hebrides islands for the time being. Samuel Henry had told John that the crews from some trading ships had stirred up a great deal of trouble there while trying to harvest the massive sandalwood trees that dotted the New Hebrides. Sandalwood fetched a high price in China, where it was used to make incense sticks, and some captains would stop at nothing to get their hands on the wood. If the islanders tried to stop the sailors from cutting down their trees, they were beaten or killed. Now, no ships were welcome in the Pacific islands far to the west of them.

While this certainly was not the way John had originally planned for things to work out when he left Raiatea, all agreed that the new arrangement would help everyone in Polynesia hear about God as quickly as possible. And that was the most important thing of all for the missionaries.

After two productive weeks at Tongatapu, the *Messenger of Peace* sailed north for Samoa. Fauea and his family were on board, and the more time John spent with them, the more impressed he was with their faith.

The voyage to Samoa was the worst John had ever encountered. Storm after storm buffeted the ship, shredding her mainsail and snapping the rigging. To make matters worse, just about everyone on board came down with influenza, which made them too weak to man the ship properly. Much to everyone's relief, the sun eventually shone again and the *Messenger of Peace* limped on.

As they neared Samoa, John and Fauea sat on deck eating dried coconut.

"You look worried," John commented.

"I am trying to maintain my faith," Fauea replied, "but I have a single great concern in returning to the land of my fathers."

"What is that?" John asked.

"In Samoa we do not have *maraes* or worship idols as do the people on other islands. We worship the spirits of the fishes and the birds. But there is a man in Samoa whose name is Tamafainga. This man has very strong evil powers, and he goes about the islands doing great wickedness and inciting the people to kill and eat each other. All of the chiefs obey him, and he might attempt to do great harm to anyone who brings the message of peace. Not that I am afraid," he added hastily. "If my blood, and the blood of my family, is shed in the name of Jesus, then so be it, but it would be a great loss for all those who will not hear the gospel."

Admiration filled John as he looked at his Samoan friend. "We will have to pray for a miracle then," he said quietly.

Chapter 12

# Samoa

After they had been at sea seven days, the cloud-capped island of Savai'i came into view, though many on the ship were still too sick to climb out of their bunks and see it. John and Charles decided to find safe anchorage so that everyone could rest on board rather than go ashore right away. They sailed around the island to the leeward side, where, as soon as they had found a safe anchorage and dropped anchor, five small canoes were pushed off from the beach and paddled out toward it. Yelps of surprise were heard as several of those paddling the canoes recognize Fauea.

"Yes, it is me, Fauea, who is the relative of Malietoa," Fauea yelled at them. "I have come back from Tongatapu on board this praying ship to tell you about the one powerful and true God. What news do you have of my relatives?"

A volley of questions and answers flew back and forth, and then John watched as Fauea proudly called his wife and children to line up along the railing. "And where is Tamafainga?" Fauea asked in a trembling voice.

"Oh!" shouted one delighted man. "He is dead, he is dead! He was killed only ten days ago, and the people are very happy!"

*Surely no happier than Fauea!* John thought as he saw his Samoan friend leap up and down shouting, *"Ua mate le Devolo. Ua mate le Devolo!"* (The devil is dead. The devil is dead!)

But the paddlers of the canoes had even more startling news. "We knew you would be coming," one of them yelled.

The statement puzzled John, as he had only changed plans in Tonga. There did not seem to be any way these people could have been warned of the arrival of the *Messenger of Peace.*

"Ask him what he means," John told Fauea.

"Why do you say that?" Fauea asked.

"It is simple," the Samoan man replied. "On the last full moon our chief lay dying. He gathered many men around him and said, 'I am leaving you now, but very soon after I go a great white chief will come from beyond the distant horizon, and he will cause the worship of spirits to cease in Samoa, and you shall know the One Great Spirit.'"

The hairs on the back of John's neck stood on end when he heard this.

The conversations continued until it was nearly dark, and that night John was so excited he could hardly sleep. He had encouraged Fauea to believe that God would perform a miracle in Samoa, and He had performed two! The ship had arrived at the perfect time. Tamafainga was dead and the chiefs had not yet appointed another "holy man," and a dying chief had given an astonishing prophecy of their arrival in Samoa.

The following morning the *Messenger of Peace* proceeded westward around the island toward the largest village, Sapapalia. The ship faced a strong head wind, and progress was made slower by the crew's exhaustion and the shredded mainsail.

In the afternoon Fauea asked to speak to John and Charles alone, and the three of them met in the ship's main cabin.

"What is it you want?" John asked.

"I have been thinking long and hard about how to bring news of God to my islands, and I have a request to make of you. I would like you to ask the Polynesian missionaries who come ashore with me not to begin their stay in Samoa by condemning our canoe races, our dances, and other amusements. The people are very much attached to these pastimes, and I worry that at the very outset they might learn to dislike a religion that places so many restraints on them. Instead, tell the missionaries to be diligent in teaching the people, to make them wise, and then their hearts will be afraid and they themselves will put away that which is evil. Let the Word prevail and get a firm grip on them, and then we can safely suggest changes that if suggested too soon would prove to be an obstacle."

"Of course we shall impress this message on the other missionaries," John assured Fauea, amazed and grateful at how thoroughly this Christian man had thought through his task.

On Sunday the ship dropped anchor in a sheltered bay, where those on board held a worship service. Once again eager Samoans paddled out to the ship, this time with goods for barter and women who were willing to come on board and entertain the men. After their initial reaction at seeing Fauea again, they offered to bring the women and trading goods on board.

"No, no," Fauea yelled at them. "This ship is a praying ship. We do not have men on board who want to be with your women. And it is our sacred day, so we will not trade goods with you until tomorrow. But you are welcome to come aboard."

The Samoans talked among themselves for a moment and then came alongside the ship and tied up. As they reached the deck, each one greeted Fauea with a hearty nose rub. Fauea invited them all to sit on the quarterdeck. John listened intently as Fauea explained to them their mission and how a number of islands, including Tahiti, Rarotonga, and Tongatapu, had given up their old gods and become Christian. John savored the moments. Taking place before him was what he had worked so hard to achieve—Christian Polynesians from one island taking the gospel to the next island. How much simpler it was for the Polynesians to receive the gospel from a fellow islander than to hear it from someone as foreign as a white man!

This thought was underscored when Fauea finished speaking and the Samoans turned their attention to John and Charles. John stood cheerfully as they fingered his shirt and examined his belt. Then one daring man bent down and pulled off John's shoes. As John stood there in his socks he heard the man whisper to Fauea, "What extraordinary people the *palangis* [white people] are. They do not have toes like we have!"

"Oh," laughed Fauea, "did I not tell you that they wear clothes on their feet? Feel them and you will find that they have toes just like us."

Much to John's amusement the men came up one by one and felt his toes. Each man gave a happy exclamation as he confirmed for himself the fact that *palangis* had toes.

On Tuesday the *Messenger of Peace* dropped anchor off Sapapalia and was quickly greeted by people paddling canoes loaded with coconuts, pigs, and bananas to sell. However, Fauea's presence on the ship created an uproar. Men swarmed onto the deck of the ship. One of the first on board was Fauea's cousin Tamalelangi—brother of Malietoa, the head chief of Samoa.

Tamalelangi was delighted to see his long-lost relative and announced that all of the produce on his canoe was no longer for sale; it was a gift to the men who had brought Fauea and his family safely back to them. The men in the other canoes followed his example, and soon the deck was covered with fresh fruit and squealing pigs.

Everything was going so well that John and Charles thought it would be safe for eight of the Polynesian missionaries to go ashore with Fauea. Their only concern was that Malietoa and his warriors were on the nearby island of Upolu avenging the death of Tamafianga. However, Tamalelangi assured everyone that the fighting would not shift to Sapapalia.

"Look," Tamalelangi said to John, pointing across to Upolu in the distance. "I see a plume of smoke rising from there. Surely my brother is gaining the victory. The smoke is no doubt from a village he has burned to the ground. I will send a messenger to fetch him, for he will want to greet you himself and talk with Fauea."

Fauea and the eight other missionaries went ashore. Later that afternoon a beautiful canoe made from the tightly laced-together skins of breadfruit paddled out to the ship. On board was Malietoa himself. "Greetings to you all!" he shouted as he came near.

John liked Malietoa right away. He seemed straightforward in his speech and actions, and he had a great deal of curiosity.

As night fell, Malietoa climbed back into his canoe, promising to visit the ship again in the morning with more produce. During the night, however, the *Messenger of Peace* drifted with the current. By the time John got up the following morning, the ship was alone in the vast ocean with not an island in sight. John estimated that they could not be more than ten or twelve miles from land, and since the water was unusually calm, he decided to take the rowboat ashore.

Six men, four Polynesians along with John and Charles, set out at nine in the morning. By lunchtime John was getting a little worried that they had not spotted land yet. By three o'clock the boat was leaking badly and there was still no sign of their destination. Because it was too late and too risky to go back hoping they could find the *Messenger of Peace,* they kept rowing straight ahead.

Finally, around sunset, the mountains of Savai'i came into view over the horizon, and soon the whole island was visible. Everyone in the rowboat was relieved when a large war canoe set out from the island to meet them and escort them ashore. A huge bonfire blazed on the beach, and as soon as the boat made it to shallow water, a group of men and boys leaped into the water to drag it to shore.

"You are the first white people ever to set foot on Savai'i," Fauea said as he greeted John and Charles on the shore.

"Well, it's not hard to see we are an oddity!" John replied as he looked around. In an effort to catch a glimpse of the two Europeans, many of the islanders had climbed to the tops of the surrounding coconut trees.

"Malietoa wishes to see you," Fauea said. "We will take you to him."

On hearing this, a number of the Samoans dipped dry coconut fronds into the fire to make torches that they used to light the way as they escorted the visitors to their chief. Men with spears and clubs parted the dense crowd ahead of them. They whacked anyone on the head who got too close to the missionaries!

John soon became separated from Charles, but he was not alarmed. Everyone seemed friendly and helpful. In fact, John quickly found out just how helpful the people were when he told one of his escorts that he was tired from rowing the boat all day. The man uttered a couple of words, and suddenly John felt people grabbing his arms and legs as he was hoisted into the air. "We will carry our honored and fatigued visitor the rest of the way," the escort announced.

Half a mile later, John was gently lowered to the ground and reunited with Charles, who'd had to walk the whole way.

The two men found themselves in the presence of Malietoa. Seated cross-legged beside him on a finely woven mat was a woman. John assumed her to be his principal wife. Malietoa greeted the missionaries and asked them to visit him again in the morning when they were rested. With that, he bid them good-night.

John and Charles were given a *fale* (hut) on the beach in which to stay. The red glow of a bonfire flickered through its woven walls, and the sound of waves gently breaking on the reef lulled John off to sleep.

The next morning John was up in time to watch a Samoan woman make his breakfast. First she took some very young coconuts and poured the milk into a wooden bowl. Then she crushed up the white meat of the coconut and mixed it in with the milk. After that she fetched a hot rock from a fire pit and dropped it into the bowl. A few minutes later the coconut soup was piping hot, and John enjoyed drinking it from a coconut shell cup.

John noticed that the woman had a pattern of dark spots all over her arms and legs, something he had not seen before. "How do you make dark spots like that?" he asked.

The woman looked a little startled by the question, but she soon answered. "When someone in our family dies, we take a piece of our cloth and twist it tight like this," she said, miming the action with her hands. "Then we set fire to it and press the burning cloth against our skin. Soon water forms underneath the skin, and when it is gone, a dark spot remains. The women with the most spots have had the most losses."

When he got back to his *fale,* John took out his journal and noted why the women blistered their bodies and how the coconut soup was made and heated. John was fascinated by the differing Polynesian customs and the way in which the people on the various islands made use of the materials available to them. He noted that, unlike the Tahitians, the Samoans did not make clay cooking pots. Since they had no fireproof pots to put directly over a fire, all liquids, it appeared, were heated with hot rocks.

Soon the village was bustling with activity, and John and Charles, along with Fauea and the missionaries with him, were escorted back to Chief Malietoa for a series of talks. They all met in a huge oval building, much superior in craftsmanship to anything John had seen in the islands. The rafters were made from the wood of the breadfruit tree and were so finely fitted together that he could not see the joints. This impressed John greatly because the Samoans did not have iron axes or tools to work with, only stones and sharks' teeth.

Gifts were exchanged, and then Malietoa and Tamalelangi officially welcomed everyone to their island and promised that they would protect the missionaries and their families. John was pleased with the way things were going. He felt confident that the Raiatean and Aitutakian missionaries he had brought with him would be safe in Samoa.

When John walked back to the beach, the *Messenger of Peace* was just coming into view over the horizon. By evening it was once more at anchor in the bay, and the Polynesian missionaries aboard, along with their wives and children, were all transported ashore.

A week later, just as the *Messenger of Peace* was preparing to set sail, a long canoe paddled into the lagoon. On board was Matetua, chief of neighboring Manono Island. He had heard that Savai'i had Christian teachers and had come to fetch some for his island. Regrettably, there were no spare missionaries to send back with him, but John promised to return with more missionaries as soon as he could. Samoa, it seemed, was ripe for the gospel.

After a long series of farewells, John and Charles boarded the *Messenger of Peace*. It seemed empty now that they had dropped off over thirty Polynesian missionaries on Savai'i. However, they had picked up eight passengers—tiny black bats, the only mammals native to the island.

John was anxious to get back and tell Mary all the wonderful things that had happened in Tongatapu and Samoa. However, the wind did not cooperate with them, and it took two weeks for the *Messenger of Peace* to cover three hundred miles. As a result they began to run low on supplies of food and water. John decided that despite his desire to get home, it would be best for the *Messenger of Peace* to head for Rarotonga, where they could replenish their supplies before conditions on the ship became desperate.

Chapter 13

# A Time to Rebuild

After such a slow start, the *Messenger of Peace* finally caught a good tail wind and covered the eight hundred miles to Rarotonga in the remarkably short time of seven days. Good news awaited John Williams there. The epidemic had run its course, though Charles Pitman estimated that about eight hundred people had died from the disease. Those who had lived through the terrible time were in good spirits, and Buteve, the man with the withered arms and legs, told John, "Rarotonga is now Rarotonga again."

While the ship was being resupplied for the next leg of the journey home to Raiatea, John and Charles Barff visited Papeiha at the village of Arorangi and the Buzacotts at Avarua. John was pleased with the progress the missionaries were making in Rarotonga. The schools were an amazing success. Aaron Buzacott's school had about seven hundred students, while Charles Pitman's had over nine hundred. When the schools in Avarua opened, the first few students were given slates to write on with chalk. The supply of slates soon ran out, and the teachers handed out trays of sand for the children to write in with a stick. These sand trays proved clumsy, and the children soon decided to make their own slates. After school they would go up into the hills and chisel out flat slabs of rock from huge boulders. They carried the slabs to the beach and rubbed them with sand and coral until they were perfectly smooth. Next they used the purple juice of mountain plantains to stain the rock slabs purple. This made the slabs look almost identical to the slates that came from England. The boys would make wooden frames to hold the mock slates while the girls went in search of sea eggs.

With their homemade slates under their arms, the children would walk to school with their heads held high. For pencils they used the spines of the sea eggs burned at the end to make them soft rather than scratchy. With these slates the children were able to form small, neat letters.

When it was time for John to leave, the Rarotongans pressed him to stay longer. John promised them that he would come back again soon and finish translating the New Testament into Rarotongan. He also said that he hoped to bring Mary and

Samuel with him. This made the Rarotongans very happy.

As they set out once again, the winds were in their favor, and the *Messenger of Peace* covered the distance to Moorea in fifteen days. In Moorea John was reunited with Mary and Samuel and John Jr. After two days of John's reporting on all of the exploits of the *Messenger of Peace* to the missionaries and the church, the Williams family made the final leg of the journey home to Raiatea.

In Raiatea the Williamses received an enthusiastic welcome. Because John had been away for so long, many of the Raiateans were convinced he had been shipwrecked. They were overjoyed to see that he was safe and to hear about the amazing story of the trip to Samoa.

Sadly, Chief Tamatoa lay ill, and John went to visit him. Many people, including his son who would be the next chief, were crowded around Tamatoa as he lay on a woven mat. John sat beside him, and the old chief reached out his hand to John. "My dear friend, how long we have labored together in this good cause; nothing has ever separated us. Now death is doing what nothing else has done, but 'who shall separate us from the love of Christ?'" Then he raised his head and spoke to the gathering. "I exhort you all to be firm in your attachment to the gospel, to maintain the laws made in this land, and to be kind and generous to our missionaries. Beware, lest the gospel be driven from these islands!"

With these words spoken, Chief Tamatoa closed his eyes and drifted from consciousness. As John watched his old friend take his last breaths, he thought back to when he first met Tamatoa. The chief had come to the island of Huahine asking that missionaries come to Raiatea and present the gospel to his people. John had accepted the challenge, and he and Tamatoa had become close friends over the years.

The Smiths, whom the LMS had sent to assist John, had arrived in Raiatea while John was gone. Now that John was back he planned to train them to take over the missionary work on the island so that in a year or so he would be free to move with his family to Rarotonga.

On September 21, 1831, convinced that the Smiths were ready to take over the work on Raiatea, John, Mary, fifteen-year-old John Jr., and four-year-old Samuel boarded the *Messenger of Peace* bound for Rarotonga. Mary had to be helped aboard because she was expecting another baby sometime after Christmas.

As the ship sailed into the small harbor at Avarua on Rarotonga, John was impressed with how neat and tidy everything looked. A sturdy coral-block wall surrounded the new gleaming white schoolhouse and chapel, and for about a mile on each side stretched houses complete with flower gardens. Once ashore, however, John learned that things were not as orderly as they looked from the boat. Some of the Rarotongans had announced they were going back to their old ways and taunted the missionaries.

John did his best to help rectify this situation, speaking at churches and villages all over the island about the need to stay true to Christian principles. The Williams family was staying and speaking at the village of Ngatangiia on the eastern side of the island when on Wednesday, December 21, four days before Christmas, the winds began to pick up. Soon driving rain was washing over the island, and still the wind increased in intensity. Coconut palms bent until they snapped in two, and roofs began to fly off the houses. Rarotonga was in the direct path of a hurricane. John hurried across the island to secure the *Messenger of Peace,* which sat at anchor in Avarua. Once he had secured his ship, he hurried back to Ngatangiia. When he arrived, he found the house the family had been staying in destroyed. Thankfully, Mary and the children had escaped and were taking refuge with the village chief. The roof on his house had been roped down to hold it in place, and the chief's house was one of the few in the village to survive the hurricane intact.

When the hurricane finally subsided two days later, John made his way back to Avarua, where he found utter devastation. Many of the trees had snapped off at ground level, crops were ruined, and not a single building in the village had survived. The new church and school lay in ruins, and worse, the *Messenger of Peace* was nowhere to be found. John finally located the vessel across a swamp and stuck in a hole in the middle of a glade of chestnut trees several hundred yards inland. The locals told him that the vessel had been carried on the crest of a tidal wave that swept across the area.

Recovering the ship would have to wait, however. The most important thing was to start rebuilding the more than one thousand smashed houses and other buildings on the island. John dispensed axes, adzes, and saws among the chiefs on the island, and the job of rebuilding began.

Five days after the storm had struck, Mary gave birth to a son. The child was stillborn, and the following day John stood with Mary, John Jr., and Samuel at the graveside as they buried the child. This on top of the devastating hurricane was almost more than John and Mary could bear, and more so because it was the seventh child Mary had given birth to that either was stillborn or had died soon after birth. Just before the coffin lid was closed, Samuel sobbed out loud, "Father, Mother, why do you plant my little brother in the ground? Don't plant him! I can't bear to have him planted."

Tears streamed down John's face. After the funeral John was too distraught to give his full attention to comforting the Rarotongans in their losses from the hurricane. In the end it was an old Rarotongan man whose words comforted John. At a service the following day, the man stood up and said, "True, our food is all destroyed, but our lives are spared, and our wives and children have escaped. Now our large new chapel is a heap of ruins, and for this we grieve most of all. Yet we have a God to worship. Our schoolhouse is washed away, yet our teachers are spared to us." The man then held up the well-worn pages of the Book of Acts. "And we still have this precious book to instruct us," he added.

John knew that the man was right. He had lost a son, but God had spared them from a worse calamity—they could all have perished in the storm. It was time to rebuild, not mourn.

During the next three months, John and Aaron Buzacott spent their mornings working on a translation of the New Testament into Rarotongan and their afternoons helping with the rebuilding of the church and school. The islanders were able to undertake much of this work themselves, since many of them had helped to build the original buildings.

Once the church and school were rebuilt, John turned his attention to retrieving the *Messenger of Peace* from its perch high and dry on the island. He used a series of wooden levers to lift the boat out of the hole amid the chestnut trees. Laboriously he filled in the swamp that lay between the glade of trees and the beach with rocks and laid logs on top of the rocks to slide the ship across. Slowly, bit by bit the vessel was skidded back toward the water until once again it was floating in the ocean. By May repairs had been made and the *Messenger of Peace* was again ready to set sail.

Once the ship was seaworthy, John and Aaron set out in it for Tahiti. Their mission was to bring back food for the people of Rarotonga. Because of the damage the hurricane had done to the trees and crops on the island, the food supply was fast running out.

The church and the missionaries in Tahiti were glad to see John. They had heard about the devastating hurricane from passing ships. And word that pieces of a medium-sized ship had been found floating near the Samoan islands had fueled speculation that the *Messenger of Peace* had gone down in the storm and all aboard her had perished. When the ship they had given up for lost dropped anchor off the island, the people were overjoyed.

Although John had planned to go straight back to Rarotonga after the ship had been loaded with food, rumors he heard on Tahiti convinced him to visit Raiatea. John headed for the island, leaving Aaron on Tahiti to work with fellow missionary David Darling on printing the portions of the Bible they had recently completed translating into Rarotongan.

An astounding sight greeted John when he stepped ashore in Raiatea. Three men from the church swaggered down the beach to greet him. They were obviously drunk! As he walked through the village, John saw children who had been enrolled in school now running around while their mothers lay inebriated on the doorsteps of their houses.

John hurried to find Edward Smith. "What has happened to the people?" he asked when he found him, although he was afraid to hear the answer.

"I'm sorry you have to see this," Edward replied. "You must be amazed. I can hardly take it in myself, and I was here when it happened."

"What happened?" John asked.

"The *Sobel* dropped anchor in the bay, and young Chief Tamatoa insisted on trading coconuts for a cask of spirits. Everyone started drinking the liquor, and the place went wild! The ship's captain showed the chief how to make a still and produce his own liquor. Now there are twenty stills on the island providing a constant supply of cheap alcohol that even some of the deacons cannot resist!"

"And how have you been fighting this?" John asked.

"It's not easy. In fact, I haven't really made much headway at all. The people seem to want to drink the stuff, and there's not much I can do to stop them."

John took a deep breath and held his temper. He had to remember that this was a new missionary he was dealing with. "Let me see what I can do. This has to stop or the people will be ruined," he replied.

John went straight to work. He called a church meeting to discuss the matter. Many of the Christians looked sheepishly at John as they walked into the chapel. From their greeting alone, it was easy for him to tell who had succumbed to the "demon alcohol" and who had stood firm in their faith.

As John began to speak, many of the Raiateans hung their heads in shame. "We have been wrong," they said. "We do not know what we were thinking."

John challenged the people that if they were truly sorry they would elect a new judge who would pass a law banning stills on the island. And that is what the people did. Old Chief Tamatoa's daughter Maihara, who lived on an outlying island, did not agree with her brother's stand on alcohol. When the new law was passed, she dispatched several men from the island to make sure every still on Raiatea was destroyed. Many people wanted the stills to stay, but Maihara was persistent, and within a week the island's source of liquor had disappeared.

Before leaving Raiatea, John had several long talks with Edward Smith about what to do when unruly ships stopped in at the island. He then headed back to Tahiti to pick up Aaron and the food supplies for Rarotonga.

Chapter 14

# A Day of Turning

Much to John's relief, Aaron had everything ready for loading when the *Messenger of Peace* arrived at Tahiti. There were twelve Yorkshire cows and two bulls and about the same number of horses and donkeys to transport. An American ship had passed by, and Aaron had bought several barrels of flour from it. This was all loaded onto the *Messenger of Peace,* along with breadfruit, taro, and dried coconut. It was hoped that all this food would tide the Rarotongans over until their own crops grew once again. As well, Aaron had acquired the old printing press that William Ellis had brought to the island, along with a stockpile of paper.

The *Messenger of Peace* set sail for Rarotonga, and when the vessel arrived, word quickly spread that John had brought back with him strange, oversized pigs. The islanders had seen a cow before on board a passing ship, but they gathered nervously as the horses and donkeys were brought ashore. No one would come near the animals at first, though the people had a long discussion about what to call them. John listened with interest as they settled on *e buaka apa tangata* (the great pig that carries the man) for the horse and *e buaka taringa roa* (the pig with long ears) for the donkey.

The missionaries kept most of the animals for breeding purposes, but they decided to butcher and eat one of the cows. The three wives set to work preparing a traditional English meal, or as close to it as they could get. The roast beef was served up with great ceremony. John carved off thick slices for everyone, although the smell of the meat made his stomach turn.

Several minutes after the meal was served, Sarah burst into tears.

"What's the matter?" Mary inquired.

"I don't like it!" Sarah replied. "All these years I've been longing for roast beef, and now I've lost the taste for it. Its flavor is too strong." She started sobbing again and then added, "What kind of barbarian have I become that I do not like roast beef?"

"I can't eat it either," Aaron confessed, "though I was not going to say anything."

In fact, not one of them wanted to eat the beef, and the meat was collected and fed to the cats.

Now that everything seemed to be under control in Rarotonga, John decided to head for Samoa again. He had promised he would return there within a year, but the hurricane had altered his plans, and now over eighteen months had passed. John planned to take a strong Christian convert named Teava along to fulfill his promise to Matetau, the chief of Manono. Chief Makea announced that he was coming on the voyage as well.

At sunset on October 11, 1832, the *Messenger of Peace* glided out of Avarua harbor under full sail. The wind stayed strong, and the ship was able to cover eight hundred miles in five days. As day broke on October 17, Manu'a, the most easterly island of Samoa, came into view. As they neared the shore of the island, several canoes approached the ship. One of the paddlers stood up and shouted, "We are sons of the Word. We are waiting for a ship of God to bring us some workers of religion. Are you such a ship?"

John was amazed. As far as he knew, no missionary of any race had ever visited this remote island. When the islanders came on board, John asked them how they had become Christians. It turned out that some Christians from Raivavae, located among the Astral Islands, about three hundred miles to the south, had been driven off course in their canoe several years before. They drifted aimlessly for nearly three months, during which time twenty of them died. Finally the few remaining survivors reached Manu'a and settled among the local people. The Raivavae Christians set up a chapel, and Hura, their teacher, carried eight pages of Scripture with him. These pages were the Raivavae castaways' most precious possession. Hura read them to their hosts, many of whom stopped their warring ways and became Christians.

"Now," one of the men explained to John, "we need a worker of religion to tell us more things of God and to show us where we are walking crooked."

John hated telling these eager converts that even though the *Messenger of Peace* was a missionary ship, he did not have any worker to leave with them. However, he promised to bring a missionary for their island back with him on a return visit.

The ship continued on to Tutuila, where it dropped anchor in Leone Bay. As John lowered the lighter over the side and headed for shore, a number of men raced down the beach and stood under a huge breadfruit tree. They looked wild, and John asked the rowers to stop. It was time to pray!

When he had finished praying, he noticed that a tall man was wading out toward them. "Son," the man shouted, "will you not come ashore? I am Chief Amoamo. Will you not land among us? We are not savage now! We are Christians."

"You, Christians?" John yelled back. "Where did you hear about Christianity?"

"A great chief from the white man's country named Williams came to Savai'i about twenty moons ago and placed some workers of religion there. Several of our people heard the workers of religion speak, and when they returned to our island they began to instruct their friends in the way. Now many of us have become sons of the Word." The chief then lifted his arm and pointed to shore. "See, there are fifty of us Christians come to greet you. You will know who we are because we have white cloth tied around our arms."

John peered at what he thought were wild islanders. The islanders did indeed have white bands on their arms!

"Why," John said, "I am the person you talk of. My name is Williams. It was I who took the workers to Savai'i twenty moons ago."

As soon as Amoamo heard this, he motioned to the group on the beach. In unison they sprang into action, running into the water and swimming out to John's boat. Once they reached it, they pulled it ashore and gathered around John.

"Do you have a chapel?" John asked, still trying to gauge how much they understood of the gospel.

Amoamo pointed to the left, and as John followed his direction he saw a small open building surrounded by banana trees.

"And who performs the services in the chapel?" he asked.

"I do," said a young man stepping forward. "See that little canoe along the beach? That is my canoe, in which I paddle over to the teachers in Savai'i. I get some religion there, and I bring it carefully home and give it to the people. And when it is gone, I take my canoe again and fetch some more. Give us a man full of religion that I may not expose my life to danger by going on so long a journey to fetch it."

The young man looked at John so expectantly that John hardly had the heart to tell him there was no missionary on the ship he could leave on the island. For the second time, all he could do was promise to return later with a missionary.

When the ship reached the island of Manono, Chief Matetau was delighted that John had returned bringing Teava and his family to be their missionaries. The *Messenger of Peace* then sailed on to Savai'i, where John had dropped off Fauea and the other Polynesian missionaries from Raiatea and Aitutaki nearly two years before.

The missionaries and their wives wept for joy as they embraced John and Chief Makea. "We have had a difficult time," they told him. "Yet we have brought some into the church of God."

As soon as supplies for the missionaries were unloaded from the ship, John heard all about their problems. Chief Malietoa was a man who loved to fight, and after the *Messenger of Peace* had sailed away, he had intensified his war against the people of Upolu. This had led to many people on both sides being killed or captured. The inhabitants of Savai'i appeared to like watching their captives die slow, painful deaths. About six months before, they had lit huge bonfires and thrown all of their prisoners—men, women, and children—into them. They then danced to the agonized screams of those perishing in the flames.

Still, the missionaries reported that many Samoans said they would give up their old ways and become Christians if and when John returned. This was great news to John, and the following morning a meeting was called. One of the Raiatean missionaries rose to address the seven hundred or so people who gathered for the meeting.

"Friends," the missionary began, "for a long time past we have been subjected to ridicule and reproach by some of you. You have said much evil against us. Here is our minister, Mr. Williams, for whom you said you would wait. You can now ask him any question that you please about the truth of what we have told you. Mr. Williams is from the fountain of truth, England. He, with his brother missionaries, is the fountain from which all true knowledge in these seas has come. Now ask him about all the points where you have doubted our word. He is our root."

No one said a word. The presence of John Williams was enough to convince them. After a few moments of silence, Malietoa rose to his feet. "Teachers," he began, "you should not regard how the ignorant among us have goaded you. From this time on let each of us put away all evil and suspicion of one another. For now, surely, you all are convinced that what you have heard is true. Let Savai'i and let all Upolu embrace this great religion. For my part, my whole soul shall be given to the word of

Jehovah, and I will use my utmost endeavors so that the word of Jehovah might encircle the land."

When the meeting was over, the Polynesian missionaries came to John. "We are so happy you came back," they told him. "Now the people can see that Christians are people of their word. Surely this day is a day of turning for Savai'i."

The following day was equally encouraging. Over one thousand people crowded into the church to hear Chief Makea of Rarotonga address them. He looked very dignified dressed in a white shirt that Sarah Buzacott had made for the occasion. Instead of trousers he wore a finely woven mat secured around his waist with a rope. The room fell silent as he stood up.

"In the time since the missionaries came to us," the chief said in a slow, deliberate voice, "we enjoy happiness, to which our ancestors were strangers. Our ferocious wars have ceased, our houses are the abodes of comfort, we have property like the white man. We have books in our own language, our children can read, and above all we know the true God and the way of salvation by His Son, Jesus Christ. I exhort you, Chief Malietoa and your brother chiefs, to grasp with a firm hold the word of Jehovah, for this alone can make you a peaceable and happy people. I myself would have died a savage had it not been for the gospel."

"We are one, we are one," Malietoa replied. "We are thoroughly one in our determination to become

Christians." Then he turned to John. "Our wish is that you should fetch your family and come and live and die with us and tell us about Jehovah and teach us how to love Jesus Christ."

For a moment John didn't know what to say. He could not live on every island he visited. Finally he spoke. "I am only one, and there are eight islands in Samoa alone. The people are so numerous that the work is too great for any one person. Here is my proposition to you. I will return immediately to my native country and inform my brother Christians of your desire for instruction. They will come to your aid."

Malietoa fixed his gaze firmly on John. "Then go, go with speed. Obtain all the missionaries you can, and come again as soon as possible."

Later that night John thought about his promise. Even though he had not voiced his desire to return to England before now, he had been thinking about it for some time. The time was right for a flood of new missionaries in the Pacific islands, and the LMS was sending out only a trickle. If John went home, maybe he could stir up interest in the Pacific and bring many missionaries back with him.

John had one other reason to think about a trip to England. John Jr. had grown into a young man. He had lived his whole life on remote Pacific islands, and it was time for him to make his own choices about where he wanted to live and what he wanted to do. For him to do this, he needed to see what England was like. Such a trip would be good for Samuel as well. He was a smart young boy who loved to learn, and it would be good for him to attend English school for a while.

By the time the *Messenger of Peace* sailed from Samoa for Rarotonga, John knew that it was the right time for him to visit England. What he did not know was that within twenty-four hours it would be doubtful whether he would make it back to Rarotonga, much less England!

Chapter 15

# Old England

"Wake up! Wake up! The ship is sinking!"

John rubbed his bleary eyes and looked into the terrified face of the first mate.

"The ship is filling with water."

John scrambled from his bunk and made his way into the hold. Sure enough, four feet of water was in the bottom of the ship. "Quick!" he ordered. "Wake everyone on board. We need to man the pumps and start bailing."

John and three of the men worked the handles of the two bilge pumps. Back and forth they went, frantically driving the pumps as fast as they could go. Meanwhile the rest of those on board formed a bucket line and started bailing water out of the hold and over the side. On they went for two hours, and in that time the water level inside the ship dropped six inches. They kept pumping and bailing until the sun began to rise. By eight o'clock their arms throbbed, but they had managed to get most of the water out of the ship. But when they stopped bailing, water began to pour back into the vessel.

The men manned the pumps again while John frantically searched below deck for the leak, but he could not find where the water was coming in. They were in a precarious situation, and he decided to take some precautions in case he couldn't find the leak. There were two rowboats on the ship into which he loaded several bags of crackers, some bamboo canteens filled with water, and some coconuts. If the *Messenger of Peace* sank, they would take to the rowboats and hope to have enough food and water to sustain them long enough to make it to an island.

John, along with everyone else on board, was tired. His arms felt like jelly, but he could not afford to stop pumping. The ship limped on for another day until some islands appeared on the horizon. They headed for the islands. At least if they sank there, they would be in shallow water and close to land. And they hoped to be able to inspect the hull from the outside while in shallow water.

They brought the ship close to one of the islands, and while the pumps were worked in shifts, three of the Polynesian men dived into the water and swam under the ship several times inspecting the hull. Still they could not find the leak.

John was unsure of what to do. Should they try to make it home to Rarotonga? Should they head for some other island group? Or should they abandon the ship, let it sink, and wait to be rescued? The next morning John still did not know what to do. Finally he decided to send the men into the water again to search for the leak. This time they were successful. In the stern of the ship, just below the rudder, they found an auger hole about two inches in diameter. The hole had apparently been drilled in the wrong place when repairs were made to the ship's rudder after the hurricane in Rarotonga. A stone had been wedged into the opening, making it watertight, but it had somehow dislodged, allowing water to now pour into the vessel. Once the hole was plugged, the ship was pumped dry and the *Messenger of Peace* set out once again for Rarotonga.

They arrived back in Rarotonga in January 1833, and within two weeks Mary Williams gave birth to yet another baby. It was another boy, and this time the child survived. John and Mary were elated to have a third healthy son. They named him William Aaron Barff Williams, or Billy for short.

As it turned out, there were several obstacles to overcome before the Williams family could sail for England. In February another devastating hurricane swept through Rarotonga, tossing roofs into the air and uprooting trees. John and the other missionaries once again set about helping to rebuild. Then John made a trip to Moorea to pick up Daniel Armitage, an expert weaver whom the LMS had sent to teach the Polynesians how to weave cloth. During this trip the *Messenger of Peace* was driven off course by a gale, and it took three weeks to get back on course.

Finally, in October 1833, John, Mary with Billy in her arms, Samuel, and John Jr. stood on the deck of the *Sir Andrew Hammond,* a whaling ship that had stopped at Tahiti to take on more provisions on her way to England. The Williams family had made their way to Tahiti to await such a ship, and to pay for their passage home, John had sold the *Messenger of Peace.* It had not been easy letting her go, but John had a glimmer of hope that while he was away in England, he might be able to raise enough money to purchase a larger vessel. Maybe then, he told himself as he watched the island of Tahiti disappear over the horizon, he could extend his work farther westward in the Pacific to the New Hebrides, the Solomon Islands, and even New Guinea.

Eight months later, in early June 1834, the Williams family arrived in Gravesend, on the River Thames. John and Mary were finally back in England after having been away for nearly eighteen years.

The family was soon caught up in a flurry of activity. Uncles and aunts wanted to meet the children. The Mission Board of the London Missionary Society requested a personal report on the South Pacific. And the boys were eager to take in all the sights around London, including Windsor Castle and the Tower of London. It was such a foreign place to them after having lived in the islands and villages of Polynesia all their lives.

By August they had settled into a house in London's Bedford Square, where they entertained many guests. John also set out to tour Great Britain. His goal was to recruit many more missionaries for the Pacific and raise the money needed to support them. At first this was an uphill battle. Few people outside of the London Missionary Society had even heard of John Williams. Eventually, though, John's persistent personality and imagination-stirring props, including bags of discarded idols and necklaces decorated with human teeth, began to draw crowds to hear him speak. Also, people loved to hear him speak in the Rarotongan language.

John's talks appealed to a wide range of people. When he spoke at a Sunday school, he told the children, "There are two little words in our language that I always want you to remember: *try* and *trust*. You do not know what you can do until you try, and if you trust God through your trials, mountains of imaginary difficulty will vanish as you approach them, and doors will open up that you could never have imagined."

After one round of speaking engagements, John came back to London to meet with members of the British and Foreign Bible Society. "We have been reviewing your work on the Rarotongan New Testament," a professor of classical languages told John, "and before we publish it, we have a few questions about your methods. To begin with, can you tell us exactly where you received your education?"

"If you are referring to where I learned to read and write, I attended school in Lower Edmondton for two years. However, I have never stopped learning since that time, although I am as apt to learn something while sitting under a tree as I am in a classroom."

"I see," replied the professor dryly. "So are we to believe that the LMS engaged your services without requiring that you attend seminary?"

"Yes," John said, frustrated that they seemed to be questioning his abilities. "The need for missionaries was great, and still is, I might add. I learned to be a missionary on the field."

"Well, that poses a problem. You see, we cannot publish a translation that is not thoroughly grounded in the original Greek text. I am sure you can understand that. Accuracy is everything."

John looked down at his hands; his knuckles were turning white. "I quite agree," he said as calmly as he could, "and I have taken great pains in comparing the translation to the original Greek. Some of us, such as yourselves, have received a classical education, and others of us have by dint of perseverance acquired sufficient knowledge of Greek to discover, by the use of good critical skills, the sense of the sacred writings."

"Do you mean to tell us you taught yourself Greek?" another member of the society asked.

"I did indeed," John replied.

"We will get back to your knowledge of Greek in a moment, but what about the orthography of Rarotongan? What text did you follow to help you decipher that language?"

John laughed. "There is no text on that. It was a process of listening to and imitating the Rarotongans until I understood what they were saying."

The questioning continued all morning until the members of the society were satisfied that John knew Greek and that his translation methods were sound. Only then did they agree to print the New Testament in Rarotongan.

When John wasn't touring the country, he translated other things into Rarotongan to be printed, including *Pilgrim's Progress* and many hymns.

After they had heard John speak, many people encouraged him to write down his story. He began to write *A Narrative of Missionary Enterprises in the South Seas.* Writing the book took a lot longer than he had anticipated, but eventually, in April 1837, it was published. John dedicated the book to King William IV and had one copy of the book elaborately bound for his wife. Inside the front cover he wrote:

> My Dearest Mary,—More than twenty eventful years have rolled away since we were united in the closest and dearest of earthly bonds, during which time we have circumnavigated the globe; we have experienced many trials and privations, while we have been honoured to communicate the best of blessings to multitudes of our fellow creatures. I present this faithful record of our mutual labours and successes as a testimony

> of my unabated affection, and I sincerely pray that if we are spared twenty years longer, the retrospect may afford equal, if not greater, cause for grateful satisfaction.
>
> John Williams

Eventually copies of the book found their way into over thirty-eight thousand homes, and as a result of reading it, many people sent donations for the LMS work in the South Pacific. Soon enough money had come in to pay for the LMS's pet project, a school for training Polynesian missionaries that was to be established in Rarotonga.

Once the money for this project was set aside, John approached the board about buying a large ship. The timing proved right. By now the board members of the LMS had seen the remarkable effect John had on his audiences and the way he threw himself wholeheartedly into every event. Even those members who had been staunchly against the LMS owning its own ship had to admit that under John's direction a ship would be a powerful tool. Indeed, through his exploits with the *Messenger of Peace,* John had already demonstrated what an indispensable part a ship played in spreading the gospel across the Pacific.

John was elated when in early 1838 he learned that the London Missionary Society had approved his proposal to raise money for a ship. He went right to work using every approach he could think of to raise money. On March 15, 1838, John even appeared before the London city council to ask for a grant. Many of the councilmen had read his book, and they voted to donate five hundred pounds to him. More money flowed in, and soon John had collected thirty-five hundred pounds—more than enough to buy a ship. John knew just the vessel he wanted. Called the *Camden,* it was a large, two-masted ship. John knew it would be just right for his needs, and he knew the man he wanted at the helm of the new ship—Captain Morgan.

John had encountered Captain Morgan many times as he crisscrossed the Pacific Ocean in the command of various ships. He was impressed with both the captain's ability to pilot his ship through dangerous waters and his Christian character. However, when John contacted Captain Morgan, the captain had just signed a contract to command another ship and was on his way to India.

This outcome disappointed John greatly, but other things encouraged him. The purchase of the *Camden* went smoothly, and the vessel was refitted. The shipbuilder did the refitting for free as his contribution to the mission. The freshwater supplier was also generous. He put twenty tons of filtered water on board the ship and refused to take money for it.

While all of this was going on, Mary was quietly preparing to leave England once again. She and John had decided to leave Samuel in London with friends. Samuel was now enrolled in school and loved learning from the classics. John was eager for him to get as much education as he could. In the meantime John Jr. had married Caroline Nichols, a girl from Linton, and the couple had committed themselves to sailing back to Rarotonga with the rest of the family.

Others planned to sail on the *Camden* when it left for the Pacific as well. John's preaching had stirred up many volunteers for the mission, and eighteen new missionaries for the South Seas were trained and ready for service.

In late March John received a letter marked "urgent" from Captain Morgan. The ship he had been aboard had been wrecked in a violent storm, and he was now able to take up the position on the *Camden* if it was still available. John was delighted. He'd had a lot of difficulty finding just the right captain for the ship and had not yet signed up anyone for the position. He immediately wrote back to Captain Morgan, asking him to report for duty.

On Wednesday, April 4, 1838, the Williams family were invited to Whitefield Tabernacle, near City Road in London, for a farewell service. When they arrived they could barely push their way through the crowd to get in the door of the church. There was not enough room inside for the hundreds of well-wishers who had shown up for the service. The crowd spilled into the street outside, where people stood quietly, joining in with the hymns and prayers.

During the service John was presented with a twenty-volume encyclopedia to take back to the islands, and then he was invited to speak. He thanked everyone for their generous support for the *Camden* and then said, "I feel, still, that the work of Christian missions is the greatest, noblest, and sublimest to which the energies of the human mind can be devoted. I think, Christian friends, that no labor we can bestow, no sacrifice that we can make, no journeys that we can undertake, are too great to be undertaken for the glorious purpose of illuminating the dark world with the light of the glorious gospel."

John spoke for twenty minutes before he concluded by saying, "Great, of course, are the perils that await me. I may not again come back to glimpse a first sight of the lofty cliffs and lovely plains of Old England; well, the will of the Lord be done! Shall I be entombed in the ocean, or sleep in a foreign land, in the Isles of the South, in the field of my labors, and among the graves of my children, time alone can reveal the will of Heaven. I will wait for that revelation in the spirit of holy submission, love, and obedience."

By now the *Camden* had been tied up at the West India dock in London, and for a week the vessel was open for people to tour. Thousands poured through the ship in that time, and then on April 9 it was moved downriver to Gravesend, where livestock and other gifts were loaded aboard for the voyage.

April 11, 1838, the day of departure, finally arrived. The LMS had chartered a steamer named the *City of Canterbury* to transport the departing missionaries and about two hundred well-wishers from London Bridge down the Thames to Gravesend.

On the trip downriver, John and the other departing missionaries said their personal goodbyes to family and friends, and a brief church service was held. At Gravesend the steamer pulled alongside the *Camden,* and the missionaries transferred on board. John helped Mary and Billy onto the ship and walked to the railing. When he looked over at the steamer, he could not see his son Samuel. "Where is Sam?" he yelled. A friend lifted the boy high in the air, and Samuel waved to his parents.

The sails of the *Camden* were unfurled, and the vessel moved off down the Thames toward the sea. Tears welled up in John's eyes as he took a last look at his son on the steamer. He was proud of Samuel, and although he knew it was the right thing to leave him behind in England, it was still very painful to do so.

John slipped his arm around his wife's waist. "Mary," he said, "Jesus says that he that loveth father or mother, sister or brother, wife or children or lands more than Him is not worthy of Him. I pray we are found worthy of Jesus and that our dear, precious boy will take hold of the grace of God so that when we return to England, we shall find our beloved boy not only intelligent and amiable but also pious and devoted, enjoying the good opinion and affection of all who know him and living in the fear of God."

"Yes, indeed," Mary said, burying her head in John's shoulder.

The *City of Canterbury* accompanied the *Camden* about ten miles before turning back for London. John stood watching it fade into the distance and reminding himself how good it felt to be back on a ship, with the smell of salt in his nostrils and the sound of breakers in his ears.

Chapter 16

# They Have Killed Our Father!

"Land ahoy!" yelled the lookout.

John and nine of the new missionary recruits who happened to be on deck at that moment rushed to the railing and peered across the deep blue ocean.

"Home at last!" John exclaimed as he spotted the mountainous peaks of Upolu rising out of the sea. He took a deep breath. How wonderful it was to be back in the South Pacific. Four years was too long to be away.

The *Camden* sailed to Fasetootai, on Upolu, which John soon decided to make his next mission base. He had originally intended to return to Rarotonga, but on the journey from England he decided to establish a new base of operations farther west.

From there it would be easier to sail the *Camden* on to the unreached islands of the New Hebrides, the Solomons, and New Guinea.

The local population was glad to hear that the Williams family was about to set up home among them and immediately built them a large temporary hut. Everyone on board the *Camden* helped unload the Williamses' belongings and settle the family into their new house. When this was done, John left Mary, Billy, and John Jr. and his wife, Caroline, behind in Samoa and set out to escort the other missionaries to their new posts.

The first port of call was Rarotonga, where John was delighted to be reunited with so many old friends. Aaron and Sarah Buzacott were thrilled to receive the five thousand New Testaments in Rarotongan. One of the first jobs for the new missionaries arriving in Rarotonga would be to help distribute the New Testaments.

John had a special embrace for Chief Makea. "Oh, Makea," he said to the chief, "how kind are God's dealings with us in sparing us thus far and permitting us to meet again."

That night a meeting was called. John closed his eyes during the singing of the first hymn. How long he had waited to hear the Rarotongan Christians singing in their strong, four-part harmony. *This is how the angels must sound,* he told himself.

Over the next week, John and Aaron worked out the plans for the new missionary training college. Aaron was eager to begin work on the structure and readily agreed to be the new school's first principal.

With these details taken care of, John was ready to reboard the *Camden*. He and the other missionaries who were sailing on to the Society Islands sent all their baggage back to the ship on the afternoon of February 11, 1839. They planned to spend one last night on Rarotonga and board the ship first thing in the morning.

Things did not go as planned, however. John awoke to the sound of a howling wind. He quickly dressed and ran down to the water's edge. The horizon was unbroken—the *Camden* was gone. John hoped that this was because Captain Morgan had put out to sea to keep the ship from being driven onto the reef by the high winds. John and the other missionaries had to wait three long weeks to find out that this was indeed the case. It was not until March 5 that Captain Morgan was able to get back to Rarotonga.

Finally the *Camden* left Rarotonga, this time with everyone on board who was supposed to be on board, and sailed on to Tahiti, Raiatea, Atiu, and Aitutaki before heading back to Upolu on May 2. Everywhere John stopped he saw signs of progress in the church—and the occasional setback as well. In Samoa a Wesleyan missionary named Peter Turner had arrived and was busy setting up a Methodist church, despite the fact that the Wesleyans and the LMS had agreed that the London Missionary Society would take responsibility for Samoa. When challenged on this fact, Peter refused to move. He even spread a rumor that John Williams had died and would not be returning, which greatly upset many of the Samoans.

Nearly four months had passed by the time John got back to Upolu. He was proud to inspect the house that John Jr. and the islanders had built for the family to live in. The place was sixty feet long and thirty feet wide and had nine rooms.

"It seems there is something of great interest to our island friends in every one of these rooms!" Mary said with a twinkle in her eye.

John laughed. "They are as curious about the things we brought back from England as the English were about the artifacts we brought from Polynesia. What is it that particularly intrigues them?"

"Well, they all bounce up and down on our four-poster bed!" she exclaimed. "And they love the patchwork quilt on the bed. Last week a group of women chided me for not wearing it to church, they thought it was so pretty. Many islanders have also walked miles to see the 'amazing likenesses.'" She pointed to the portraits of Samuel and other members of the family that hung in ornate frames on the wall. "They ask if it is possible for me to make the portraits speak to them! Oh, and you must see them looking in the mirror. It is large enough for twenty or more of them to see themselves at once, and they come in and get up to the funniest antics in front of it. They grin and stare, then dance and jump. Poor Caroline has a never-ending job trying to keep the sand and dirt out of the house, but having an open house is so worth it. Every week we make new friends and invite them to chapel."

"How wonderful," John said as Billy raced into the house.

"Papa, Papa, come and see my room!" Billy yelled. "I have a window all to myself, and a collection of sea eggs."

John was delighted to see how well everyone had settled into the new home.

With so many novice missionaries scattered on the surrounding islands, John had plenty of work to keep him busy, but his heart was never far from the voyage west. Eventually, after John had been back in the Pacific islands for ten months, he felt the time was right to make the trip. A full moon glittered on the ocean as John said good-bye to Mary and the rest of his family. Hundreds of Christians gathered on the beach at midnight as John, twenty Samoan missionaries, and James Harris, a young Christian man from England who had come to Samoa to observe the work of the LMS for himself, were paddled out to the *Camden*. It was November 3, 1839, and John expected to be away for several months.

The *Camden* stopped in at Apia, farther along the coast of Upolu, where Nicholas Cunningham, a young adventurer and recently appointed British vice consul in the area, asked if he could join them on the trip west. John agreed, and they journeyed on to several mission stations on Savai'i before heading west for Rotuma.

John hoped to leave two Polynesian missionaries on Rotuma to set up a halfway station between Samoa and the New Hebrides. However, the Rotumans proved very unfriendly. The women and children jeered at the ship and threw sticks and stones into the water. Several men did go ashore, but the head chief refused to meet with them, and everyone on the *Camden* felt it was best to make a quick exit.

The next island they visited was Futuna, the most easterly island in the New Hebrides. The people who lived on these islands were not Polynesian but Melanesian. Their skin color was darker than that of the Polynesians, and their language was very different. The chief of Futuna was much friendlier than the chief on Rotuma had been. He presented the missionaries with food and gestured that he would be willing to have a missionary live among them at some later date.

From Futuna the *Camden* sailed on to the island of Tanna, where the missionaries were greeted with cautious friendliness. John was very impressed with the potential of this island as a mission station, and he left two of the Samoan missionaries there, promising to check up on them on the return voyage.

It was early morning on November 20 when the *Camden* cut its way through the sea on the south side of the island of Erromanga. John watched from the deck as a canoe containing three men paddled out from the shore. "Lower the boat," he said to Captain Morgan. "We shall go and meet our new friends."

Soon the rowboat was lowered, and John, Captain Morgan, Nicolas Cunningham, James Harris, and four Polynesian rowers climbed in and headed toward the canoe.

"We greet you as friends," John yelled in Samoan. He knew they would not understand what he said, but he hoped his tone would convey a certain friendliness.

The men in the canoe did not answer. Instead they looked shyly away and headed back toward the beach.

"What do you think?" John asked the others. "Should we follow them?"

"Look, there are boys on the beach now. That's a good sign. Islanders put children out of the way when they are plotting an attack, don't they?" Nicolas asked.

"That's true, but where are the women? I'd be much happier if I could see them as well," Captain Morgan replied.

The conversation went back and forth as the canoe got closer to shore. Everything looked normal as the three men pulled their canoe up onto the beach.

"Let's go," John said. "The other islanders we've met have been shy, too."

A few minutes later the rowboat was just offshore. Several Erromangan men ran along the rocks toward them, and John threw out some beads, hoping to set their minds at ease. Then he held up some fishhooks and a small mirror, motioning for the men to come and get them. When they did not, the four white men in the boat climbed out and waded ashore.

John reached out to shake hands with the first Erromangan he came across, but the man ran away.

"They certainly are shy," Captain Morgan remarked.

Even so, the islanders did show signs of friendliness. They fetched water for the men and opened coconuts for them to drink. In return John gave them cloth and the other goods he had with him.

All appeared to be going well when James said, "I think I'm going to walk up the beach a little and stretch my legs." As he walked, six Erromangan men followed him.

"I think I'll walk a bit, too. How about you?" Nicolas said to John.

"Good idea," John replied.

With that the two men walked down the beach a little way while Captain Morgan and the Samoan rowers stayed near the boat.

Again several island men followed them. John held up five fingers and started to count in Rarotongan. He hoped the men would catch on and count out loud in Erromangan so that he could hear how different the words were.

Nicolas stopped to pick up a shell from the beach when suddenly he and John heard a shout. James came sprinting out of the bushes.

Nicolas dropped his shell and yelled, "Run for the boat."

John hesitated for a second and then dashed for the sea. He was a good swimmer, and he hoped that the boat would pick him up in the water. Three men wielding clubs were close on his heels.

Crack! John felt the thud on the back of his head. Searing pain shot through him as he stumbled on. Then everything went black. His head fell forward, and he collapsed at the water's edge.

"Hurry," Captain Morgan yelled to Nicolas. He grabbed Nicolas's jacket and heaved him onto the bottom of the boat as soon as Nicolas was close enough. "Go! Go!" he ordered the rowers.

The four rowers pulled on the oars with all their might, and the boat slipped away from the beach. Several of the Erromangan men pursued them, but not for long.

As the rowboat headed for the *Camden,* Captain Morgan looked back. The islanders were stripping the bloodied bodies of John and James. "God have mercy on them," he said.

Everyone was crowded onto the deck of the ship, waiting to hear what had happened.

"We have lost Williams and Harris," Captain Morgan yelled up to them. "They are dead. The natives have killed them."

One of the Polynesians began to wail, and soon others joined in. "Our father! Our father! They have killed our father!"

Captain Morgan ordered the sails be hoisted as soon as he was aboard the *Camden*. He maneuvered the vessel as near to the shore as he dared and fired a shot into the air, hoping to scare away the islanders. Instead of running from the slain bodies, the men dragged them away into the bushes. There was little more anyone could do, and so with a heavy heart Captain Morgan set a southeasterly course. They would sail to Sydney and request a navy ship be sent to recover the remains of the two men.

That night Captain Morgan read a portion of John's diary to everyone aboard. John had penned some words the day they sailed away from Rotuma. "We live in a dying world," the entry began. "Ere long some friend will communicate to surviving relatives the information of our death. The grand concern should be to live in a constant state of preparation. I am all anxiety but desire prudence and faithfulness in the management of the attempt to impart the gospel to these benighted people and leave the event with God."

On November 30, 1839, the *Camden* arrived in Sydney bearing its grim news. And on February 1, 1840, the warship HMS *Favourite* was available to return to Erromanga. Nicolas Cunningham went along on the ship to show the captain the spot where the two men had been murdered.

Eventually the captain of the *Favourite* was able to make contact with the Erromangans, and through a series of hand signals, he learned that the bodies of John and James had both been eaten. The islanders offered two skulls and some bones, which they claimed belonged to the men, but there was no way to know whether they were telling the truth.

From Erromanga the HMS *Favourite* sailed on to Samoa, where Mary Williams and her children had already heard the news of John's death from Captain Morgan. A funeral service was held, and the bones of John Williams were buried in Apia, Samoa. A memorial stone was placed on top of the grave. It read, "Sacred to the memory of Rev. John Williams, Father of the Samoan and other missions, aged 43 years and 5 months, who was killed by the cruel natives of Erromanga, on November 20, 1839, while endeavouring to plant the Gospel of Peace on their shores."

George Pritchard, one of John's old missionary friends and now British consul to Tahiti, wrote about John's death in a letter to a friend. In it he tried to explain why the Erromangans were so hostile to the missionaries.

> In this case, as in most others, the foreigners have been the first aggressors. A few years ago, several foreigners united, chartered vessels, and went with an armed force, took possession of a part of Erromanga, built a fort to protect themselves, and then cut, at their pleasure, the sandal wood belonging to the poor natives. This sandal wood is very valuable in the China market. After obtaining a considerable quantity, a disease broke out among them which carried off a great many; the others were compelled to leave; many of the natives were killed by them.

> I am not sure that Mr. Williams knew that this was the island where the sandal wood expedition had been; but there is no doubt his death, and that of Mr. Harris, was in consequence to the base treatment the natives had received from the foreigners who forced their way upon these shores.

The Williams family stayed on in Samoa for two years, after which time Mary decided to return to England with Billy. She settled in Islington and attended Union Chapel there until her death in 1851.

The careers of each of John's sons reflected a part of his own calling. John Jr. spent the rest of his life in the South Pacific, where he was at various times both the American and the British consul. Samuel became a Congregational minister in England, while Billy set up a publishing business there.

In life John Williams inspired many young Polynesians to go as missionaries and take the gospel to neighboring islands. After his death this did not stop. The missionaries continued with the pattern John had set, and Polynesians continued to be sent out to the islands of the Western Pacific until Christianity was finally spread all the way to New Guinea. John Williams's vision had come to pass; like links in a chain, the gospel now stretched across the Pacific Ocean.

# Bibliography

Ellis, James J. *John Williams: The Martyr Missionary of Polynesia*. S. W. Partridge & Co.

Garrett, John. *To Live Among the Stars: Christian Origins in Oceania*. World Council of Churches/University of the South Pacific, 1982.

Gutch, John. *Beyond the Reefs: The Life of John Williams, Missionary*. Macdonald and Company, 1974.

*The Life of John Williams, Missionary to the South Seas, An Abridgement of "Missionary Enterprises in the South Sea Islands" by John Williams*. Revivalist Press, 1915.

Matthewman, Phyllis. *John Williams*. Zondervan Publishing House, 1955.

Tippett, Alan R. *People Movements in Southern Polynesia: A Study in Church Growth*. Moody Press, 1971.

## *About the Authors*

Janet and Geoff Benge are a husband and wife writing team with more than thirty years of writing experience. Janet is a former elementary school teacher. Geoff holds a degree in history. Originally from New Zealand, the Benges spent ten years serving with Youth With A Mission. They have two daughters, Laura and Shannon, and an adopted son, Lito. They make their home in the Orlando, Florida, area.

Christian Heroes: Then & Now are available in paperback, e-book, and audiobook formats, with more coming soon!

**www.YWAMpublishing.com**

# *Also from Janet and Geoff Benge...*

More adventure-filled biographies for ages 10 to 100!

## Christian Heroes: Then and Now

*Gladys Aylward: The Adventure of a Lifetime* • 978-1-57658-019-6
*Nate Saint: On a Wing and a Prayer* • 978-1-57658-017-2
*Hudson Taylor: Deep in the Heart of China* • 978-1-57658-016-5
*Amy Carmichael: Rescuer of Precious Gems* • 978-1-57658-018-9
*Eric Liddell: Something Greater Than Gold* • 978-1-57658-137-7
*Corrie ten Boom: Keeper of the Angels' Den* • 978-1-57658-136-0
*William Carey: Obliged to Go* • 978-1-57658-147-6
*George Müller: Guardian of Bristol's Orphans* • 978-1-57658-145-2
*Jim Elliot: One Great Purpose* • 978-1-57658-146-9
*Mary Slessor: Forward into Calabar* • 978-1-57658-148-3
*David Livingstone: Africa's Trailblazer* • 978-1-57658-153-7
*Betty Greene: Wings to Serve* • 978-1-57658-152-0
*Adoniram Judson: Bound for Burma* • 978-1-57658-161-2
*Cameron Townsend: Good News in Every Language* • 978-1-57658-164-3
*Jonathan Goforth: An Open Door in China* • 978-1-57658-174-2
*Lottie Moon: Giving Her All for China* • 978-1-57658-188-9
*John Williams: Messenger of Peace* • 978-1-57658-256-5
*William Booth: Soup, Soap, and Salvation* • 978-1-57658-258-9
*Rowland Bingham: Into Africa's Interior* • 978-1-57658-282-4
*Ida Scudder: Healing Bodies, Touching Hearts* • 978-1-57658-285-5
*Wilfred Grenfell: Fisher of Men* • 978-1-57658-292-3
*Lillian Trasher: The Greatest Wonder in Egypt* • 978-1-57658-305-0
*Loren Cunningham: Into All the World* • 978-1-57658-199-5
*Florence Young: Mission Accomplished* • 978-1-57658-313-5
*Sundar Singh: Footprints Over the Mountains* • 978-1-57658-318-0
*C.T. Studd: No Retreat* • 978-1-57658-288-6
*Rachel Saint: A Star in the Jungle* • 978-1-57658-337-1
*Brother Andrew: God's Secret Agent* • 978-1-57658-355-5
*Clarence Jones: Mr. Radio* • 978-1-57658-343-2
*Count Zinzendorf: Firstfruit* • 978-1-57658-262-6
*John Wesley: The World His Parish* • 978-1-57658-382-1
*C. S. Lewis: Master Storyteller* • 978-1-57658-385-2
*David Bussau: Facing the World Head-on* • 978-1-57658-415-6
*Jacob DeShazer: Forgive Your Enemies* • 978-1-57658-475-0
*Isobel Kuhn: On the Roof of the World* • 978-1-57658-497-2
*Elisabeth Elliot: Joyful Surrender* • 978-1-57658-513-9
*D. L. Moody: Bringing Souls to Christ* • 978-1-57658-552-8
*Paul Brand: Helping Hands* • 978-1-57658-536-8
*Dietrich Bonhoeffer: In the Midst of Wickedness* • 978-1-57658-713-3
*Francis Asbury: Circuit Rider* • 978-1-57658-737-9
*Samuel Zwemer: The Burden of Arabia* • 978-1-57658-738-6

*Klaus-Dieter John: Hope in the Land of the Incas* • 978-1-57658-826-2
*Mildred Cable: Through the Jade Gate* • 978-1-57658-886-4
*John Flynn: Into the Never Never* • 978-1-57658-898-7
*Richard Wurmbrand: Love Your Enemies* • 978-1-57658-987-8
*Charles Mulli: We Are Family* • 978-1-57658-894-9
*John Newton: Change of Heart* • 978-1-57658-909-0
*Helen Roseveare: Mama Luka* • 978-1-57658-910-6
*Norman Grubb: Mission Builder* • 978-1-57658-915-1
*Albert Schweitzer: Le Grand Docteur* • 978-1-57658-961-8

## Heroes of History

*George Washington Carver: From Slave to Scientist* • 978-1-883002-78-7
*Abraham Lincoln: A New Birth of Freedom* • 978-1-883002-79-4
*Meriwether Lewis: Off the Edge of the Map* • 978-1-883002-80-0
*George Washington: True Patriot* • 978-1-883002-81-7
*William Penn: Liberty and Justice for All* • 978-1-883002-82-4
*Harriet Tubman: Freedombound* • 978-1-883002-90-9
*John Adams: Independence Forever* • 978-1-883002-50-3
*Clara Barton: Courage under Fire* • 978-1-883002-51-0
*Daniel Boone: Frontiersman* • 978-1-932096-09-5
*Theodore Roosevelt: An American Original* • 978-1-932096-10-1
*Douglas MacArthur: What Greater Honor* • 978-1-932096-15-6
*Benjamin Franklin: Live Wire* • 978-1-932096-14-9
*Christopher Columbus: Across the Ocean Sea* • 978-1-932096-23-1
*Laura Ingalls Wilder: A Storybook Life* • 978-1-932096-32-3
*Orville Wright: The Flyer* • 978-1-932096-34-7
*Captain John Smith: A Foothold in the New World* • 978-1-932096-36-1
*Thomas Edison: Inspiration and Hard Work* • 978-1-932096-37-8
*Alan Shepard: Higher and Faster* • 978-1-932096-41-5
*Ronald Reagan: Destiny at His Side* • 978-1-932096-65-1
*Davy Crockett: Ever Westward* • 978-1-932096-67-5
*Milton Hershey: More Than Chocolate* • 978-1-932096-82-8
*Billy Graham: America's Pastor* • 978-1-62486-024-9
*Ben Carson: A Chance at Life* • 978-1-62486-034-8
*Louis Zamperini: Redemption* • 978-1-62486-049-2
*Elizabeth Fry: Angel of Newgate* • 978-1-62486-064-5
*William Wilberforce: Take Up the Fight* • 978-1-62486-057-7
*William Bradford: Plymouth's Rock* • 978-1-62486-092-8
*Ernest Shackleton: Going South* • 978-1-62486-093-5
*Benjamin Rush: The Common Good* • 978-1-62486-123-9
*Dwight Eisenhower: Supreme Commander* • 978-1-62486-142-0
*Frederick Douglass: The Right to Dignity* • 978-1-62486-151-2
*Winston Churchill: Resolute* • 978-1-62486-153-6

Heroes of History are available in paperback, e-book, and audiobook formats, with more titles coming soon! Curriculum Guides are also available for all U.S. biographies.

www.heroesofhistory.com